The Ladder
of the
Beatitudes

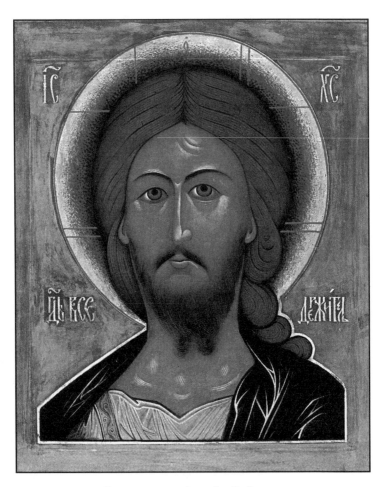

Contemporary icon by Sofronov

The Ladder
of the
Beatitudes

Jim Forest

ORBIS BOOKS

Maryknoll, New York 10545

Fourth printing, May 2003

The Catholic Foreign Mission Society of America (Maryknoll) re-cruits and trains people for overseas missionary service. Through Orbis Books, Maryknoll aims to foster the international dialogue that is essential to mission. The books published, however, reflect the opin-ions of their authors and are not meant to represent the official posi-tion of the society.

Manufactured in the United States of America.
Copy editing and typesetting by Joan Weber Laflamme.

Library of Congress Cataloging-in-Publication Data

Forest, James H.
 The ladder of the Beatitudes / Jim Forest.
  p. cm.
 ISBN 1-57075-245-1 (pbk.)
  1. Beatitudes–Criticism, interpretation, etc. 2. Spiritual life–Christianity. I. Title.
 BT382.F67 1999
 241.5'3–dc21   98-47780
                                                                  CIP

✤

Blessed are the poor in spirit, for theirs is the kingdom
    of heaven.
Blessed are they who mourn, for they shall be comforted.
Blessed are the meek, for they shall inherit the earth.
Blessed are they who hunger and thirst for
    righteousness, for they shall be satisfied.
Blessed are the merciful, for they shall be shown mercy.
Blessed are the pure of heart, for they shall see God.
Blessed are the peacemakers, for they will be called
    children of God.
Blessed are they who are persecuted for the sake of
    righteousness, for theirs is the kingdom of heaven.
Blessed are you when they insult you and persecute
    you and utter every kind of evil against you falsely
    because of me.
Rejoice and be glad, for your reward will be great in
    heaven, for so men persecuted the prophets who
    were before you.

—MATTHEW 5:3-12

for Anne

Contents

Contents

Introduction

This book began nearly twenty years ago during a stay on the Island of Iona.

On a map of Great Britain, Iona is that bit of land about the size of an apostrophe just off the southwest tip of Mull in the Inner Hebrides. You can walk Iona's circumference in a day if you start early, though some parts are rugged. The island has been a goal of pilgrims for nearly fourteen hundred years, having been the base of Saint Columba's community.

I dare to hope that Columba would give his blessing to these pages.

One of the great saints of Ireland, this prince-turned-monk left his homeland in 563 as an act of penance for having been party to a war. It is said that he and twelve companions settled on Iona because it was the first island they came to after the last trace of Ireland disappeared over the southern horizon.

Columba was to Christianity in Scotland what Patrick had been two generations earlier to the Irish. Both taught, healed, did wonders, and spread the faith among primitive, battling peoples. Out of such leadership Celtic Christianity took root. Missionaries went out from Iona to instruct and baptize, to found communities and schools, and to win in the process such a reputation for holiness that, even in the sixth century, pilgrims came to Iona from as far away as Rome. Macbeth and other kings were buried there, as Iona was regarded as a favorable place to await the Last Judgment.[1]

Columba was a man with a powerful presence. It's said his voice could be heard a mile away. Writers admire that kind of broadcasting ability.

The earliest recorded encounter with the aquatic dragon of Loch Ness involves Columba. Having risen out of the water directly in front of the monks' coracle, the awesome creature gave way when Columba made the sign of the cross. The monks were allowed to pass without harm. Must we believe the tale? It isn't a precondition for reading this book. What is certainly true is that Columba and his fellow missionaries often risked death in order to share life in Christ with others and that doing this among the tribes of Scotland was no safer an enterprise than battling dragons.

His penance having been undertaken because of war, Columba never again had a casual attitude about violence. There is the story that on one occasion, in a moment of absentmindedness, he blessed a certain object before it dawned on him that it was a battle sword. Immediately he gave the weapon a second, more restrictive blessing: that it would be useful only for cutting cheese and bread, and that as long as it was used only for such purposes it would never grow dull.

Columba's monastic rule, eventually used by many similar communities, obliged the monks to own nothing but bare necessities, live in a place with but one door, anchor their conversations in God and the gospel, refuse idle words and the spreading of rumor and evil reports, and follow all the rules that govern spiritual life. They were to prepare always for death and suffering, offer forgiveness from the heart to everyone, pray constantly for anyone who was in trouble, put almsgiving before all other duties, not eat unless hungry or sleep unless tired, pray until tears came and labor to the point of tears—or if tears "are not free, until your perspiration flows freely."

It was a rule very like the beatitudes.

Did I know such details about Columba twenty years ago? Probably not. I had come to the island to lead a small retreat for a group of people who were about to set off on a pilgrimage that would take them across Scotland and the length of England before reaching Canterbury Cathedral on the eve of Pentecost.

What led me to focus on the beatitudes I no longer recall, only that it was the first time it dawned on me that the beatitudes have a ladder-like structure, with poverty of spirit the essential starting point and with the cross at the top. These ten verses have never been far from my thoughts ever since. What progress I have made so far in understanding them is reflected in this small book.

The process of reflection is far from over. Ten or twenty years from now, if I can still make sense of the alphabet and haven't yet moved to the cemetery, perhaps I will write a better book on the same subject. (With that possibility in mind, I invite readers to share any insights, stories, or corrections that occur to them as they read these pages. Send your letter to me in care of the publisher, Orbis Books.)

A few details about the text: Whenever using quotations, I have tried to provide an endnote, not because this is an academic work but so the reader who wishes to go further with a particular text or saint may more easily do so. No one translation of the Bible has been used, though the Authorized, RSV, the New RSV, and the NIV are among translations that have been consulted.

This book would certainly not have been written without the encouragement of my editor, Robert Ellsberg. We've been friends a long time. I treasure a photo I took of him on the roof of Notre Dame of Chartres in France twenty-seven years ago. I was not quite half my present age, and Robert was still in high school.

Though I have no one to blame for the book's shortcomings but myself, it would be a worse book had it not been for the help of many people who saw sections of it in draft, among them James Allaire, Catherine Costello, Bob Graf, Harold Isbell, Denise Jillions, Archimandrite Ephrem Lash, Daniel Lieuwen, Susan Massotty, Margot Muntz, Fr. Sergei Ovsiannikov, Fr. Patrick Reardon, Karen Redington, Ivan Sewter, Fr. James Silver, Bette Tomlinson, and Renée Zitzloff.

Most of all, I thank my wife, Nancy, for her part in bringing this project to life.

–JIM FOREST

Icon of the Heavenly Ladder of St. John Climacus

Rung by rung

Blessed is the person whose desire for God has become like the lover's passion for the beloved.

—SAINT JOHN CLIMACUS[2]

Even in a culture in which the Bible is a dark and unmapped continent to millions of people, if you say "Blessed are . . . ," someone is likely to add the next few words of the first beatitude, "the poor in spirit." The text is hard to forget, even if it isn't easily understood.

With only a little effort, all the beatitudes can be memorized. Once learned by heart, we carry within us for the rest of our lives a short summary of the teaching of Jesus Christ: the whole gospel in a grain of salt.

Some churches see to it that the beatitudes become engraved in our hearts while we are still children. In the Orthodox church it is customary to sing the beatitudes every Sunday during the first procession, when the gospel book is carried out of the sanctuary into the main part of the church and back into the sanctuary again to be placed on the altar. Week after week the words are sung until they reach so deep a place that late in life, when the face in the mirror belongs to a stranger, these words will still shine like pebbles in a stream.

Anything sung is easily memorized. The neurologist Oliver Sacks tells the story of a man who had lost every vestige of memory but could, when attending Mass, sing the entire liturgy.[3]

There are eight beatitudes, if we recognize the last two verses as one, as both describe the suffering often imposed upon those who live the gospel: eight facets of discipleship. Yet in another

1

sense, there is only one beatitude, because all are aspects of life in communion with God. Each of the eight describes aspects of being in the kingdom of God.

They are like rungs on a ladder, which Christ has arranged in an exact order. There is a pattern to his arrangement. Each step builds on the foundation of the previous step, each leads to the next, and each is indispensable. We can't divide them up, retaining those we find appealing and leaving those we don't care for to others, as if one could specialize: "I'll take peace-making, you can have purity of heart."

Saint John Climacus (c. 579-649), one of the Desert Fathers, used the same metaphor for a more complex arrangement in his *Ladder of Divine Ascent*, a strategy of salvation which begins with the renunciation of worldly life and ascends through obedience, penitence, detachment, and humility in the daily struggle to enter more and more deeply into the love of God and freedom from everything that impedes that love. So far as I am aware, his is the only book that has given rise to its own icon: the image of a ladder with many rungs stretching from the desert toward the welcoming arms of Christ in the upper right-hand corner. The ladder is crowded with those who wish to enter the kingdom of God, but they are under attack by small demons armed with arrows, spears, and robes. Succumbing to various temptations, some are shown falling off the ladder.

The Christian life is climbing the ladder of the beatitudes—and when we fall off, starting once again.

Teacher and healer

O inexpressible mystery and unheard of paradox: the Invisible is seen, the Intangible is touched, the Eternal Word becomes accessible to our speech, the Timeless steps into time, the Son of God becomes the Son of Man.

—Saint Gregory of Nyssa

To whom are we listening? This is the pivotal question of the New Testament. Is Jesus Christ simply one of the great teachers of history—someone of the stature of the Buddha, Gandhi, or Martin Luther King Jr.—or is he God incarnate? Is he a person deeply buried in the ancient past, whose life and activities happened to give rise to the religion known as Christianity? Or is he someone living? Should we speak of him in the past or present tense?

For many people, it's definitely Jesus of the past tense. Hundreds of books have been published about the long-dead Rabbi Jesus, a man more hidden than revealed by the gospels, whose real story and doctrine can only be uncovered by a rigorous process of sifting line by line through scriptural and other ancient texts, throwing out the legends and supernatural inventions until at last certain passages and stories can be certified as credible and therefore possibly genuine. Then the modern reader will have reliable information about some of the actual things Jesus of Nazareth did and said before his untimely execution and burial, events which the early church camouflaged with stories of a resurrection—a metaphor for the durability of his teaching and the way he lived on in the courage and good deeds of his followers. It is taken for granted that the miracles recorded in the gospel either didn't happen or only seemed to be miracles to the primitive people who witnessed them.

"They're stoning Jesus to death with footnotes," a friend in Boston tells me, "and doing a better job of the execution than the Romans did with the cross."

Then there are those for whom Jesus is in the present tense, Christ risen from the dead and always with us, not only alive but the source of life "in whom we live and move and have our being" (Acts 17:28). Such people—the author of this book is one of them—see the church as the conscientious guardian of the gospels and the gospels as true.

Those who wrote the New Testament would sympathize with those who find it hard to believe in the Christ of the gospels. Far from presenting their response to Christ in the best possible light, the authors of the four gospels make clear that it was no easy thing for the disciples to understand who he was. As soon as he began to teach, he was recognized as a man who spoke with a special authority, an inspired teacher, clearly a leader, possibly a prophet, perhaps the messiah sent by God to free and lead the Jews.

It was only after Pentecost, looking back over events they witnessed, that they began to understand what they had only dimly grasped at the time.

A man born blind

One of the events Saint John dwells on—it's the whole of chapter nine in his gospel—concerns a man blind from birth. A beggar, he is sitting on the Sabbath at his usual spot on a street in Jerusalem and becomes the object of a question put to Jesus as he passes by: "Rabbi, who sinned, this man or his parents, that he was born blind?" The assumption was that a disability had to be a punishment.

You have to imagine the blind man simply listening in his lifelong darkness to the exchange, curious as to what the rabbi will say. He hears an unexpected answer from Jesus: "It was not this man who sinned, or his parents, but that the works of God might be made visible in him." Then Jesus adds enigmatically, "We must do the works of him who sent me while it is day. Night comes and then no one can work. As long as I am in the world, I am the light of the world."

The blind man says nothing and asks for nothing. He makes no verbal appeal for a miracle. He is as silent as the grave.

Then Jesus, as if working on the creation of Adam, makes a paste of earth and spit, applies it to the man's tomb-like eyes, and tells him to wash his face in the nearby Pool of Siloam. The man's one act of faith is to obey the unseen rabbi named Jesus.

"So he washed and came back seeing," Saint John records. By then Jesus had walked on.

The miracle is described with economy. The main part of the chapter isn't about the healing of a blind man's eyes but about how others respond to it.

There are those who doubt this is actually the blind beggar. "Some said, 'It is he.' Others said, 'No, but he is like him.'" The man insists he is himself, then tells what happened, how a rabbi named Jesus made clay and anointed him with it and sent him to wash his face in the Pool of Siloam, and afterward he could see. They ask where this rabbi is, but the man doesn't know.

The argument becomes so heated that the disputants bring the man before a council of Pharisees, a respected group among the Jewish people for whom the careful observance of the Law of Moses had absolute priority. For them, it was obvious that Jesus was a sinner because he had made mud on the Sabbath, a form of labor, however minor, thus a violation of the Sabbath statutes prohibiting all work.

To get to the bottom of things and to reveal what they assume is an act of deception (we too tend to assume the worst of beggars), the Pharisees call the beggar's parents. They affirm that he is their son and that he was always blind. Asked how it is possible that he now has his sight, they respond, "Ask him. He is old enough. He can speak for himself." Saint John explains that the parents were afraid. We can take for granted that they were among the city's poor—otherwise their son wouldn't have had to beg. They are poor and powerless—people intimidated by lawyers.

The man was questioned a second time. Lawyers know stories don't always hold up under persistent questioning. They say to him, "Give God the glory. We know the man [Jesus] is a sinner." "Give God the glory" is similar to the proverb, "Speak the truth and shame the devil," for God is glorified whenever the truth is told and dishonored whenever the truth is denied.

The man bears witness to what has happened to him: "Whether the man who healed me is a sinner or not, I do not know. One thing I know—I was blind and now I see."

More than his blind eyes have been healed—he doesn't share the fear that afflicted his parents. When asked again how Jesus cured his blindness, he tells the interrogators that he has told them the truth, but they didn't want to hear it. "Why do you want to hear it again? Do you want to become his disciples?"

The word *disciple* must have gone off like a firecracker. Those questioning him respond, "It's you who are his disciple—we are disciples of Moses! We know God spoke to Moses but we do not know where this one is from."

The beggar is reckless in his response: "This is amazing," he says. "You don't know where he is from, but he opened my eyes." He points out the obvious—God doesn't listen to sinners but only to the devout. Now here is someone who has healed a man blind from birth, something absolutely unheard of. "If this man were not from God, he would not be able to do anything."

An uneducated beggar dares to argue with prominent and well-educated men and is rebuffed for his effrontery. "You were born totally in sin," they tell him, the assumption being that his blindness was proof of that. "Now you try to teach us!" He is shown the door.

All the while Jesus is elsewhere, but he hears what has happened and seeks out the man who had been blind. The striking thing is that once again it is Jesus taking the lead. He finds him and says, "Do you believe in the Son of Man?" *Son of Man* is a messianic title, the new Adam, the long-awaited one who would rescue Israel. The healed man responds with his own question, "Who is he, sir, that I might worship him?"

Now, with this nameless man on his first day of seeing, we stand at the absolute heart of the gospel. Jesus answers: "You have seen him and the one who is speaking with you is he."

The healed man's response is immediate. "He said, 'I do believe, Lord,' and he worshiped him."

Worship is both an attitude and a physical action. We can assume the man either fell on his knees or prostrated himself, actions mirroring the awareness that he was in the presence of the Savior.

The key verse in the narrative is Jesus saying, "I am the light of the world." In icons of Christ holding open the gospel, this verse is often the text displayed—a one-sentence summation of his identity.

The story can be read on more than one level. First of all, it is a faithful account of a remarkable event that happened one day in Jerusalem nearly two thousand years ago; but it also has to do with us. Putting ourselves in the place of the blind man, we can see ourselves as blind from birth—not blind in the sense of being unable to see the material world around us but blind in our inability to see God, blind in not noticing the Creator in creation, blind in our inability to see God's image in others. It is usually a worsening blindness; as we get older we tend to become less and less amazed, so that things which were once astonishing become ordinary. Boredom can become a constant condition, with relief being sought through distraction. We may be far less in touch with the world around us than the blind beggar who was sitting between the Temple and the Pool of Siloam.

Sitting in darkness, I happen to hear a circle of voices discussing why it is that I have this unfortunate condition. Someone is asking if it is my fault or someone else's? Who is to blame? Then I hear a voice speaking with confidence about "making visible the works of God."

I can't understand what he means. What can my disability have to do with making visible the power of God? But as the wet clay is rubbed on my face and washed off in the waters of baptismal awakening, it dawns on me that the answer is not a theory or a principle about light or enlightenment. The answer is a particular person. Jesus is not just another teacher but Christ himself, the messiah we have awaited, who reveals himself in word and action as the light of the world.

It wasn't easier to believe two thousand years ago in Jerusalem than it is here and now. This chapter in Saint John's gospel is mainly about people not believing what they themselves had seen or others had witnessed. It is a story of sighted people being blind and insisting on remaining blind. It is as if they were saying, "We see enough and know enough already. We don't need any new prophets or street-corner messiahs. We have a lifetime supply of wisdom and rules. Take your miracles and beggars and go away. We have seen enough."

To climb the ladder of the beatitudes, we need to be climbing toward the living Christ, not a dead body or an intellectual concept. Such climbing is worship, no different from the worship of the healed man who recognized Jesus as Lord. The first part of his healing was that he could see the objects and people around him, but the more important gift was that before the day was over he realized he was in the presence of the Son of Man, the light of the world, he who had shaped Adam from dirt and spit.

Matthew, the narrator

It is in Saint Matthew's gospel that we find the beatitudes.

The story of Matthew becoming one of the inner circle of Jesus' followers is briefly related in his own gospel. In the town of Capernaum on the Sea of Galilee, Jesus had just forgiven the sins of a paralytic, an action that angered the local scribes, who accused him of blasphemy. Who is this upstart from Nazareth to be absolving sins that God alone can forgive? To show he had power to forgive, Jesus healed the crippled man.

Immediately afterward Jesus "saw a man called Matthew sitting in the tax office and said to him, 'Follow me.' And he rose and followed him" (Mt 9:9).

The troubles of life are summed up in the phrase *death and taxes*. Matthew was a tax collector. While tax collection has never been a widely admired trade, in Matthew's day and place it was regarded with particular contempt. "Jews abhorred tax collectors to the extent they refused to marry into a family which had a tax collector among its members, banished them from communion in religious worship, and shunned them in all affairs of civil society and commerce," it is noted in *Butler's Lives of the Saints.*[4] Tax collectors were in the front ranks of those collaborating with the Roman occupiers. They were well rewarded for their loathsome work, retaining a percentage of all they collected and thus becoming members of the tiny class of wealthy people. The words *honest* and *tax collector* fit together at that time as much as *honest* and *used car salesman* do in ours. Tax collectors in the Roman era were regarded as grasping extortionists whose only principle was the increase of their own income. That Jesus could imagine a tax collector as an apostle is even more remarkable than the prophet Hosea marrying a prostitute. If Matthew had the makings of an evangelist, there is no one who doesn't.

Matthew was despised and knew it well. Many in Galilee must have spit on the ground at the mention of his name. Try to imagine what it was like for such a man to have the eyes of Christ rest upon him, seeing in him someone he had not yet become—a man of prayer, free of all possessions, fearless, the author of the first gospel, recorder of the sermon on the mount, a witness of the resurrection, an apostle, finally a missionary and martyr.

His home was Capernaum—a pinprick on the map but not a backwater village. Besides the tax office, a detachment of soldiers was stationed there. The town's synagogue was uncovered by archeologists early in the twentieth century—a third-century building standing where the smaller synagogue of Jesus' day had been. Among recent discoveries in the neighborhood are the remains of an ancient vegetarian restaurant—evidence that the trade routes which passed through Capernaum brought travelers not only from Egypt in the south but Hindu India in the distant east.

It may be that Capernaum had always been Matthew's home. Jesus had grown up a day's walk to the west in the village of Nazareth but moved to Capernaum to begin his mission, preaching, healing, and attracting his first disciples. Among the other apostles from Capernaum was Peter, though he was still called Simon. At the edge of town was the fishing boat Simon and his brother had been working on when Jesus summoned them as disciples. Among those healed by Jesus in Capernaum was Simon's mother-in-law. Together with Peter's wife, she probably cooked meals for Jesus on occasion.

Like everyone in the area, Matthew would have been aware of Jesus and must have been thinking about the meaning of his words and actions. Was he a prophet? Could he be the messiah? Jesus would have been the subject of countless arguments:

"Who does he think he is?"

"On the other hand, he healed Simon's mother-in-law and you know how sick she was."

"Who made you a doctor? Maybe it was all in her head. Mother, father, children—in that family they're all missing a few rafters. Look at Simon and Andrew, leaving their nets to become 'fishers of men.' Those boys don't have the brains they were born with. You can't eat weeds."

Matthew the tax collector presumably had no taste for weeds. On the other hand, like many wealthy men, he knew a good deal about what money cannot buy and how hard-won possessions become life-consuming burdens. Clearly he was ready to respond to Jesus' invitation and, like the fishermen brothers who had already been called, leave everything behind.

Beginning at the beginning

There are so many Old Testament references in his gospel that it's clear Matthew wrote his account of the Savior's life, teaching, and activities with his fellow Jews in mind. He assumes the reader is familiar with the Law and the prophets and frequently notes how actions in Jesus' life fulfill biblical prophecies.

Matthew begins at the beginning, with a family tree—Christ's human genealogy, but at the same time a history of humanity, especially the Jewish people. The first chapter also affirms that Jesus was miraculously conceived, fulfilling the words of Isaiah: "A virgin shall conceive and bear a son."

Matthew relates Joseph's obedience to an angelic voice heard in a dream. Dream-attentive, God-fearing Joseph, like his namesake of the coat of many colors, puts aside his reservations and weds Mary, though she is carrying a child he had not fathered.

Matthew provides several details of Christ's birth and infancy, relating Herod's efforts to prevent an upstart "messiah" from taking the throne. When he heard from the three wise men that they were seeking a child who would be king of the Jews, Herod sent soldiers to murder all the male infants of Bethlehem up to the age of two. Jesus only narrowly escaped the slaughter, thanks once again to Joseph obeying a dream and escaping with his wife and son to Egypt. Finally, after Herod's death, Joseph brings his wife and their son back from exile, settling a safe distance from Jerusalem in Galilee.

We also hear from Matthew about John the Baptist's activity in the Judean wilderness, which culminates in his baptism of Jesus, when for the first time in the New Testament there is a "showing" of the Holy Trinity: "And behold, the heavens opened and John saw the Spirit of God descending like a dove and alighting on Jesus, and a voice from heaven saying, 'This is my beloved Son, with whom I am well pleased.'"

Matthew describes Jesus' subsequent withdrawal into the wilderness, where he was confronted and tempted while fasting for forty days, finally dismissing Satan with the words, "You shall worship the Lord your God and him only shall you serve."

Next Matthew records Jesus leaving Nazareth to live in Capernaum, then calling the first apostles, the brothers Simon and Andrew, and two other brothers, James and John.

The fourth chapter of Saint Matthew's gospel concludes, "He went about all Galilee, teaching in the synagogues, preaching the good news of the kingdom, and healing every disease and infirmity among the people." The fame of Jesus rapidly spread in the region "and great crowds followed him."

In the first four chapters we hear very little from Jesus directly. In the next three chapters we hear *only* the voice of Christ—his sermon on the mount.

The setting

> *"Seeing the crowds, he went up on the mountain, and when he sat down his disciples came to him. And he opened his mouth and taught them."*
>
> —MATTHEW 5:1-2

"Seeing the crowds" tells us that many people were present when Jesus was teaching that day. What he had to say was for ordinary people, not just an elite inner circle. His words are for everyone and anyone. In the verses just before the sermon on the mount Matthew describes the sort of person who would have been in the crowd: "They brought unto him all the sick, those afflicted with various diseases and torments, people possessed with devils, epileptics, paralytics, and he healed them."

"He went up on the mountain." Mountains are images of earth reaching toward heaven, thus places of encounter between Creator and creature. According to tradition the "mountain" on which Jesus announced the beatitudes was a towering hill near Capernaum, an ideal place for a large gathering. While our family was picnicking near the top of that hill in 1985, admiring the sweeping view of the Sea of Galilee, we found ourselves listening to a spirited black minister from Chicago explaining the sermon on the mount to a crowd of American pilgrims. The minister must have been fifty yards away, but we heard his voice easily. It wasn't hard to imagine a much larger crowd listening to Jesus teach in the same place twenty centuries before.

In biblical significance the mount of the beatitudes is linked with a much more formidable geological monument, Mount Sinai, a remote and barren fortress of stone in the southern

Sinai desert. On the pinnacle of Mount Sinai, Moses, amid flashes of lightning in a dense cloud, talked with God and received the tablets of the Law. But there are contrasts more striking than the difference between a green hill and a pinnacle of rock. On Sinai, only Moses was permitted to come near, while in Galilee, anyone who was curious was welcome to listen to the Son of God explain the principles of living in the kingdom of God.

"He sat down." Sitting down was the normal posture of a teacher in the classical world. The attention Matthew gives to this detail indicates the teaching was formal, not casual. Similarly, in a synagogue, the rabbi sat down while delivering a sermon. In universities, certain "chairs" (faculty positions) are permanently established. The cathedral is so named because the bishop's chair—*cathedra* in Latin—is located there.

"He opened his mouth and taught them." The form renders a Semitic phrase that marks an authoritative proclamation. It is not enough simply to say, as a modern journalist would, "He taught them." More is required to reveal the gravity of the event. This is Jesus' inaugural address.

Blessed

In English the first verses of the sermon on the mount are called the beatitudes. The traditional Russian phrase is "the commandments of blessedness." The first word of each beatitude isn't an everyday word. We have to ask ourselves before going further what *blessed* and *beatitude* mean.

Beatitude comes from the Latin word *beatus,* meaning "happy, fortunate, blissful." In the context of the gods in Elysium, it meant supremely happy, in a state of pure bliss. In the late fourth century *beatus* was the word Saint Jerome opted for in his translation of the "blessed are" verses.

"I would expect that, like so many other Latin writers, Jerome was assuming that the meaning would enlarge within its textual context," Latin scholar Harold Isbell tells me. "However, don't overlook the possibility that because Greek is a more nuanced language, it conveys degrees of meaning that the hardheaded Roman would not suspect. Then there is 'beatific,' as in 'beatific vision,' which in the Christian tradition of the West refers specifically to the vision of God, an entirely appropriate but quite unmerited fruit of God's creative act."[5]

While most English Bibles use "blessed," some modern translations prefer "happy": "How happy are the poor of spirit . . . "

"'Happy' isn't good enough," Rabbi Steven Schwarzschild once told me. "The biblical translator who uses such a word should change jobs, maybe write TV comedies with nice happy endings. The problem is that, if you decide you don't like 'blessed,' there isn't a single English word which can take its place. You might use a phrase like 'on the right track' or 'going in the right direction.' Sin means being *off* the track, missing the target. Being 'blessed' means you aren't lost—you're on the path the Creator intends you to be on. But what you recognize as a blessing may look like an affliction to an outsider. Exchanging 'blessed' for 'happy' trivializes the biblical word. You might as well sum up the Bible with a slogan like, 'Have a nice day.'"

"Happy" in some respects makes for an unhappy translation. Its root is *hap*, the Middle English word for "luck." The word *happen* is a daughter word. A *happenstance* approach to life is to let things happen as they will, to depend on the roll of the dice. To act in a *haphazard* manner is to do things by chance. To be *hapless* is to be unlucky, but to have good luck is to be a winner. The lucky person, the happy person, has things going his or her way. We say certain people were born under a lucky star—they seem to get all the breaks, everything from good looks to money in the bank.

The founding fathers of the United States, in declaring independence from Britain, recognized "Life, Liberty, and the pursuit of Happiness" as unalienable rights. For them, the pursuit of happiness meant each person had the right to seek his own good fortune and not simply be the servant of another. In our era, in which happiness is somewhere between a human right and a social duty, many people feel guilty for failing to be continually happy.

But what about the word *blessed?* This was the word chosen by translators in the seventeenth century. *Blessed* meant "something consecrated to or belonging to God."

Several Hebrew words have been translated as "blessed," beginning with *baruk,* as in the verse: "And God *blessed* them [the first man and woman], saying, Be fruitful and multiply" (Gn 1:28). *Baruk* is linked to kneeling—a blessing would be received while kneeling in a posture of respect and submission.

"*Baruk* is frequently applied to God, indeed the *berakah* is the characteristic Jewish prayer," Archimandrite Ephrem Lash of the Monastery of Saint Andrew in Manchester explained to me. "The typical Jewish prayer begins, 'Blessed are you, Lord our God, . . . ' There is even a *berakah* for forgetting the correct *berakah*. This has been taken into Christianity, in particular into Orthodoxy, where no service can begin without a *berakah*–'Blessed is our God now and forever and unto the ages of ages,' or 'Blessed is the kingdom of the Father, the Son and the Holy Spirit.'"

Ashre is another Hebrew word that has been translated as "blessed." It is an exclamation–"Oh, the good fortune!" The root meaning is "to go straight, to advance." The person of whom one can say *ashre ha-ish* is one for whom things are on the right track, going along a straight way, making headway. It is often used in the book of Psalms, as seen in the first psalm:

> Blessed is the man
>   who walks not in the counsel of the wicked,
> nor stands in the way of sinners,
>   nor sits in the seat of scoffers,
> but his delight is in the law of the LORD,
>   and on his law he meditates day and night.

The next verse offers a metaphor of what it is like to be blessed–such a person "is like a tree planted by streams of water."

There is the similar Hebrew word *ashar*. In the book of Proverbs it is used in a passage describing the ideal woman:

> Her children rise up and call her blessed; her husband also, and he praises her. (Prv 31:28)

All the gospels were first written in Greek. In those passages where "blessed" is a verb, the Greek is *eulogeo* ("to bless")–an action associated with praise, thanksgiving, and consecration, and therefore used in liturgical contexts. For example:

> And as they ate, Jesus took bread and blessed and broke it and gave it to them, saying, "Take, eat, this is my body." (Mk 14:22)

Where "blessed" is used as an adjective, it is a translation of *makarios*. It is *makarios* that is used throughout the beatitudes.

We also hear it also in such texts as, "Blessed are your eyes for they see, and your ears for they hear," and, "Blessed are you, Simon Bar-Jona, for flesh and blood has not revealed this to you, but my Father in heaven" (Mt 13:16, 16:17).

In classical Greek *makar* was associated with the immortal gods. *Kari* means "fate" or "death," but with the negative prefix *ma* the word means "being deathless, no longer subject to fate," a condition both inaccessible and longed for by mortals. It was because of their immortality that the gods, the *hoi Makarioi*, were the blessed ones.

"The interesting thing about *ashre* is that it is never, so far as I know, applied to God," Archimandrite Ephrem points out. "On the other hand the Greek *makar* starts life as precisely something which the gods are, though the related adjective *makarios* is more commonly applied to humans."

In Christian use, *makarios* came increasingly to mean sharing in the life of God, the ultimate joy, a happiness without the fault lines of happenstance running through it. There is no higher gift. We are not simply capable of an abstract awareness that God exists or of studying God as an astronomer might study the night sky, all the while knowing the stars are unbridgeable distances away, that their light may be centuries old by the time it reaches our eyes, and that the objects that produced the light may no longer exist. The blessing extended to us is participation in the communion of the holy Trinity, sharing in God's immortality and being blessed with qualities that seem humanly impossible.

Blessed are the poor in spirit . . .

Blessed are they who have nothing to lock up.
—DOSTOEVSKY, *CRIME AND PUNISHMENT*

The monks of the Egyptian desert in the fourth century described some who came to visit them as "visitors from Jerusalem," others as "visitors from Babylon." It was their way of distinguishing pilgrim from tourist. The tourist is seeking new sights, a glimpse of life in another part of the world, sometimes courting adventure, or perhaps just the experience of an exotic location. The pilgrim is seeking God.

Inside Jerusalem's Church of the Holy Sepulcher (or Church of the Resurrection, as Orthodox Christians call it) my wife once found herself standing on a borderline between tourists and pilgrims while she was waiting in line to enter the tomb in which Christ was buried. Before her was an American couple who had come as part of a tour, but whose guide apparently hadn't made clear why they were being shown a small chapel under a huge dome in an ancient church. "Maybe it's where he was born," the wife said. "No," said her husband, "that was yesterday, in Bethlehem." "Oh, yes. But then what is it?" Her husband didn't know. Finally it was their turn to go inside. The wife did what she had seen others ahead of her do—kneel by a stone slab inside the narrow enclosure while her husband took a photograph. But in front of what?

Meanwhile, behind Nancy were several older Greek women, all in black, each holding a clutch of candles like a bouquet of flowers, none of them saying a word, tears streaming down their faces. They knew exactly where they were. Behind them, on what was then a small hill just outside the city walls, Jesus

Christ, God incarnate, had been crucified, while in front of them was the actual place where his dead body had been put in a sealed tomb and left under Roman guard, the place where he rose from the dead. They were inching their way toward the resurrection, history's central event, the axis on which the church's calendar turns, and with it their own lives.

In the age of tourism, how do we become pilgrims?

The answer is the day-by-day practice of poverty of spirit, the first rung of the ladder of the beatitudes. Poverty of spirit is the essential beginning, the context of discipleship. Without it we cannot begin to follow Christ.

What does poverty of spirit mean? It is my awareness that I cannot save myself, that I am basically defenseless, that neither money nor power will spare me from suffering and death, and that no matter what I achieve and acquire in this life, it will be far less than I wanted. Poverty of spirit is my awareness that I need God's help and mercy more than I need anything else. Poverty of spirit is getting free of the rule of fear, fear being the great force that restrains us from acts of love. Being poor in spirit means letting go of the myth that the more I possess, the happier I'll be. It is an outlook summed up in a French proverb: When you die, you carry in your clutched hand only what you gave away. Poverty of spirit is a letting go of self and of all that keeps you locked in yourself.

"The first beatitude," comments Metropolitan Anthony Bloom, "stands at the threshold of the Kingdom of God. . . . Blessed are those who have understood that they are nothing in themselves, possess nothing that they dare call 'their own.' If they are 'something,' it is because they are loved of God and because they know for certain that their worth in God's eyes can be measured by the humiliation of the Son of God."[6]

Poverty of any kind is little praised beyond the Bible.

"Poverty is a great enemy to human happiness," Samuel Johnson warned James Boswell, "for it certainly destroys liberty, and it makes some virtues impracticable, and others extremely difficult." Johnson only gives a fine polish to advice that has been handed down for countless generations. In one wing of my family it is summed up in a joke—"Rich or poor, it's best to have money."

"What this century worships is wealth," wrote Oscar Wilde in his play *An Ideal Husband*. "The God of this century is wealth. To succeed one must have wealth. At all costs one must have wealth."

"Food, clothing, fuel, rent, taxes, respectability and children," George Bernard Shaw has Undershaft declare in his play *Major Barbara*, "nothing can lift those seven millstones from Man's neck but money; and the spirit cannot soar until the millstones are lifted." Shaw's subject was how unbearably tempting money is even to preachers who sing the praises of poverty.

The first beatitude, pointing as it does in the opposite direction, is a permanent thorn in our sides. For twenty centuries men and women, some of them theologians, have been searching for a loophole.

One of the most popular is simply to bracket the beatitudes, along with anything else in the New Testament that seems impractical, as a "counsel of perfection," advice for monks and nuns, something for the occasional Saint Francis or Mother Teresa rather than the ordinary person. But if one can be a Christian without taking seriously the teachings or example of Christ, the word *Christian* no longer means "a follower of Christ."

Another approach has been to spiritualize the text: "Jesus of Nazareth was indifferent to material possessions. He didn't care whether or not his followers were rich or poor. It simply wasn't important. Only one thing was important—the person's *attitude*."

This approach at least has the virtue of taking the text seriously, even if shifting the stress. After all, Christ speaks of "poverty *of spirit*." Clearly attitude matters. The poverty Christ calls blessed is useless if it is resented or hated. The person who is poor but is obsessed with what he wishes he owned has become a billionaire in his fantasy life. He may be poor according to economists, but he isn't poor in spirit.

But is Jesus neutral to wealth itself and only concerned about one's attitude toward riches? When you look further in the gospels to see what else he has to say about money, you find Christ never encourages the pursuit of wealth. Elsewhere in the sermon on the mount he teaches, "But seek for yourselves treasure in heaven, where neither moth nor rust corrupt and where thieves do not break in or steal" (Mt 6:20). On another occasion he warns his disciples that it is "easier for a camel to pass through the eye of a needle than for a rich man to enter the kingdom of heaven," only adding the consoling words to his anxious listeners that "anything is possible with God" (Mt 19:24-26).

Again and again Saint Matthew, a man who had himself been wealthy, draws attention to those words of Jesus, which saved him from devoting his life to acquiring and protecting money.

The Greek word used for "poor" in the first beatitude–*ptochos*–refers not just to a person who possesses very little but to someone who is destitute. There is a different word–*penes*–for a person who has the basic necessities: no luxuries, no savings, nothing superfluous, but is not in debt. He lives from the honest work of his hands and enjoys the respect of his neighbors, while a destitute person has been reduced to begging and has, as Jesus said of himself, "no place to lay his head" (Mt 8:20).

The state of need Christ describes is urgent and absolute, the desperate condition of need of someone at the very bottom. A good translation of the first beatitude into modern English is, "Blessed are the beggars in spirit . . . "

Does the first beatitude mean that to follow Christ one has to dispossess oneself of everything and become voluntarily destitute?

That depends on what God requires. It is a life-by-life question. There is no one-size-fits-all Christian vocation.

Among the saints one easily finds those who owned close to nothing and would without hesitation give away what little they still possessed.

One of the Egyptian Desert Fathers sold his most precious possession, his Bible, in order to have alms for the poor, explaining, "I have sold the book that told me 'sell what you have and give it to the poor'" (Mt 19:21). Among the saints there are those who gave away the last stitch of clothing, becoming as naked as Adam and Eve—like Saint Basil, a "holy fool" of Moscow, after whom Russia's most famous cathedral is named.[7]

But sanctity is not the sum of the would-be saint's empty pockets. There have been many whose feats of asceticism were displays more of pride than of poverty of spirit. Early in his monastic life John the Dwarf announced to a brother that he was going deeper into the Egyptian desert, declaring that from now on he would live like an angel. Several days later, close to starvation, John knocked again on the brother's door. "Who is there?" asked the brother. "John." "No, it can't be John," said the brother. "John is now an angel—he no longer needs food and shelter." Only then did he open his door to the chagrined and hungry John. The chastened monk embraced a humbler, more ordinary poverty.[8]

The exterior forms of poverty vary from person to person and even from year to year in a particular life. Neither Christ nor the apostles went naked—we find Christ without clothing in public only on two occasions in his adult life: his baptism and his crucifixion.

Other than Christ himself, Christ's mother is the paradigm of poverty of spirit. Her unconditional assent to the will of God is a model for every Christian: "Be it done to me according to your word" (Lk 1:38). She is quietly present at every step along the way and with the apostles after Pentecost. At the marriage feast at Cana, after drawing her son's attention to the fact that there was no more wine, she instructs the servants of the feast, "Do whatever he tells you" (Jn 2:5). This is her advice to all who follow her son. Whenever we defer our will to the will of God, we open ourselves to God's transforming power, just as she did.

Dorothy Day, a saint of hospitality and a writer who often recommended voluntary poverty to readers of *The Catholic Worker*, wore hand-me-down suits and struggled to own as little as possible. "Those who cannot see the face of Christ in the poor are atheists indeed," she often said. She was distressed about the irritation she felt when her books were borrowed and not returned—"I am too attached to my library," she confessed to me more than once. The impressive thing is that this attachment did not cause her to live a life in which her books would have been less likely to disappear.

Another saint of recent times was the Russian Orthodox nun Mother Maria Skobtsova, whose house of hospitality in Paris opened its door to anyone in need. Her assistance to Jews during the time of the Nazi occupation led to her arrest and later to death in the gas chamber at Ravensbrück. She saw each person as "the very icon of God incarnate in the world" and sought "to accept this awesome revelation of God unconditionally, to venerate the image of God" in everyone in need. Her personal possessions fit into one suitcase; her bedroom was a corner in the basement.

Saint Francis of Assisi spoke of having "Sister Poverty" as his bride. "Holy Poverty," he wrote in his *Salutation of the Virtues*, "destroys the desire of riches and avarice and the cares of this world."[9] He was convinced that voluntary poverty was the only way to overcome war and give witness to the peace of Christ. Francis's robe—a patchwork quilt of rags—is still preserved at the basilica in Assisi.

Henry David Thoreau was no Christian missionary, but he had a Franciscan sensibility about the problem of wealth. As he wrote in *Walden* in the chapter on economy: "How many a poor immortal soul have I met well-nigh crushed and smothered under its load, creeping down the road of life, pushing before it a barn seventy-five feet by forty, its Augean stables never cleansed, and one hundred acres of land, tillage, mowing, pasture, and wood-lot! The portionless, who struggle with no such unnecessary inherited encumbrances, find it labor enough to subdue and cultivate a few cubic feet of flesh."

Mother Teresa of Calcutta owned two saris, a rosary, a Bible, and a few prayer books. We know her not for what she possessed but for what she did—the many years she spent creating communities to care for dying people abandoned by others and to give assistance to pregnant women under pressure to abort their unborn children. She regarded the greatest poverty not as something material but as lack of faith and being closed in on oneself.

Far more often than not saints had little personal property, and what they possessed they held lightly. Yet there are also other saints who, at least for a substantial part of their lives, possessed a great deal and lived in comfort, rarely worrying about a roof over their heads or a pillow under it. As Saint Leo the Great observed: "While it cannot be doubted that poverty of spirit is more easily acquired by the poor than the rich, for submissiveness is the companion of those in want, even in many of the rich is found that spirit which uses its abundance not for the increasing of its pride but on works of mercy, regarding as the highest profit that which it expends in the relief of others' hardships."[10]

Saint Thomas More, a chancellor of England during the reign of Henry VIII, owned a large and handsome house and was waited on by servants—until he was made a prisoner in the Tower of London. Finally he was beheaded for his opposition to the king's divorce of his first wife. He had been a generous man but not a poor one until poverty and confinement were forced upon him. More's lively spirit and inner freedom even while a prisoner are revealed in an exchange when More was being tried. Lord Rich said to him, "You know that if you won't take an oath to the King, then you are going to have to leave behind your lovely home in Chelsea and your wife and your children and it's only a question of taking an oath, otherwise you will die." More replied, "I die today, my Lord, and you die tomorrow."

One of the widely revered saints of the Orthodox church, Prince Vladimir of Kiev, led the people of early Russia to baptism in the year 988. Before his conversion Vladimir was far from saintly; Saint Nestor, in his *Chronicle,* described him as a man who had been "insatiable in vice." The Slavic people regard him as a saint not only for bringing the people of Kiev to the Dnieper River for baptism but because, following his conversion, he himself gave a heroic example of what it meant to follow Christ. He became renowned for his care of the poor, orphans, and the sick. The palace gates were opened to the hungry. He built hospices for the aged. He banned torture and executions. Yet he lived in a palace and dressed like the royalty he was.

Two of his sons, rather than shed the blood of an ambitious brother, chose to die without defending themselves. The young princes, Boris and Gleb, were the first Russians to be recognized as saints. Yet they too had been finely dressed and had known royal comforts.

One could fill a library with books about saints who lived in fine houses and had wine with their meals, and a still larger library with the lives of saints who counted it wealth to sleep on a straw-filled mattress and eat a piece of stale bread from time to time. Their superficial differences are stunning, yet when you look closely at the lives of the saints, you discover what they had or didn't have was part of their particular obedience to Christ. *All* the saints are linked by poverty of spirit. *All* the saints lived an ascetic life. *All* of them approached God in a state of destitution, seeking as a matter of life or death to know God's will in their lives and to live it, for God not only creates us but gives each of us a unique identity, a unique responsibility, a unique path to follow on the way to heaven. Poverty of spirit—the condition of being a spiritual beggar—is seeking to live God's will rather than one's own.

For most of us, our vocational obedience involves responsibility for material objects as well as earning and spending money. The vocation of parenthood involves many years of caring for children, trying to provide for both their physical and spiritual needs. Few people do not require certain tools, a place to live, and a variety of possessions. If you are a plumber or mechanic, there are tools that are essential to your work. If you are a scholar, you need a substantial library or access to one. Nor are the possessions we need only connected to our work; they may also be connected to spiritual and intellectual growth.

What is crucial is the *way* we possess what we possess, the care we take not to let possessions take ownership of our souls, and how we use what we have to express God's mercy.

The underlying questions are: What is of ultimate significance in our life? Our own comfort and reputation? Our own importance? Or the love of God and caring for those around us? One way or another, how we relate to material objects reveals who we are, the condition of our soul, and whether we are citizens of heaven or hell.

One of the great saints of the Egyptian desert, Abba Dorotheos, told a story that reveals poverty of spirit in such a way that an Alexandrian of great importance was able to grasp it:

I remember once we had a conversation about humility. One of the notable citizens of the city was amazed on hearing our words that the nearer one draws to God, the more he sees himself to be a sinner. Not understanding, he asked, "How can this be?" I said to him: "Notable citizen, tell me how do you rank yourself in your own city?" He answered: "I regard myself as first in the city." I said to him, "If you should go to Caesarea, how would you regard yourself there?" He answered, "As the least of the civic leaders there." Then I asked, "And if you should travel to Antioch, how would you regard yourself there?" "There," he answered, "I would consider myself as one of the common people." "And if," I asked, "you should go to Constantinople and approach the Emperor, how would you see yourself there?" And he answered: "Almost as nothing." Then I answered him, "So it is also with the saints. The nearer they draw to God, the more they see themselves to be sinners."

... for theirs is the kingdom of heaven.

We are joined to one another and to Christ like flour in a loaf.
—Saint John Chrysostom[11]

Notice that Christ uses the present tense, not the future—it isn't "theirs *will be* the kingdom of heaven" but "theirs *is* the kingdom of heaven." (Because of the Jewish aversion to speaking directly of the Creator as God, Saint Matthew consistently uses the phrase "kingdom of heaven." The other three gospel authors speak of the "kingdom of God." The meaning in all four gospels is the same.)

The cartoon image of heaven—a domain in the clouds whose residents, having retired from earthly existence after more-or-less virtuous lives, are rewarded with white robes, angel wings, and golden harps—is almost as uninviting as the usual stereotype of hell—a cavern in a volcano occupied by naked people being tormented by demons. At least this image of hell has a biblical basis: Christ speaks of hell as "an unquenchable fire" (Mk 9:44). But a heaven of clouds, harps, and bathrobes has no connection to the gospel.

This past summer Nancy and I found vivid imagery of heaven and hell when we camped near the town of Autun in the countryside southwest of Dijon in France. Here, in the twelfth-century Cathedral of Saint Lazarus, are some of the finest carvings made in the Romanesque era, the work of a man named Giselbertus, who left us nothing but his vision of the gospel. The most impressive carving of all is the large tympanum over the church entrance in which, within a wide half-circle, Giselbertus offers a deeply insightful vision of the Last Judgment.

Detail of the Last Judgment, Autun Cathedral

At the center, far larger than any other figure, is Christ enthroned within an angel-borne oval that gives a symbolic shape to eternity and the kingdom of heaven. His arms are opened in a simple gesture of greeting, as if saying, "Welcome, you blessed of my Father, into the kingdom prepared for you since the foundation of the world" (Mt 25:34).

The sun and moon are to the right and left of his face; Mary, his mother, is enthroned to one side; beneath her is a group of apostles. On the other side there is a large scale on which a man is being weighed while a hideous devil struggles to tilt the scale in hell's favor. Meanwhile a lithe angel in fluted robes, with the lightest touch, overcomes Satan's effort.

At the lowest level of the tympanum, beneath Christ's feet and stretching the full width of the church's central doors, is a long row of people standing on their coffins, freshly raised from the dead. A sword-bearing angel at the center of the figures looks with sorrow rather than outrage toward the wretched figures on the right, whose lives have brought them damnation. Each of the damned seems closed in on himself, fascinated with his own misery. The remarkable thing is that not one of them notices Christ. They didn't see him in life, and they don't see him in the afterlife either.

In contrast, all the saved but one are looking in enraptured amazement toward Christ; the one exception, a child, points at Christ with one hand while telling a guardian angel what he has seen.

The gospel according to Giselbertus is that we are in heaven whenever we see Christ or are aware of his presence. Heaven is participation in God's being. It is seeing what has always been close at hand, what was always at the heart of reality, but somehow was barely recognized, glimpsed "as through a glass darkly" (1 Cor 13:12).

We learn from the first beatitude that those whose treasure is God are already within the borders of the kingdom of heaven. "All the way to heaven is heaven," said the great mystic Saint Catherine of Siena, "because he said, 'I am the way.'" It is similar to the medieval proverb of pilgrims walking to holy places: If you do not travel with him whom you seek, you will not find him at the end of your journey.

"What do you mean when you speak about the kingdom of heaven?" The disciples must have asked this question often because the gospel is so full of Jesus' answers.

Christ responds with parables, one of the longest being about forgiveness. He says, "The kingdom of heaven may be compared to a king who wished to settle accounts with his slaves." The story centers on a slave who owed the king a fortune, ten thousand talents–a way of saying he owed an unpayable amount; one talent was worth more than a laborer earned in fifteen years. The king says he is going to sell the slave along with all his family and possessions, but the slave falls to his knees, begs the king's patience, and is forgiven his debt. Immediately afterward, the slave encounters a man who owes him a hundred denarii (one denarius was the wage a laborer received for day's work). The man with the smaller debt begs patience, promising he will repay, but the appeal is refused and the man is sent to prison. Hearing what happened, the king chastises the debtor he had forgiven: "You wicked slave! I forgave you all that debt because you pleaded with me. Should you not have had mercy on your fellow slave, as I had mercy on you?" The enraged king orders the unforgiving man punished until his own debt is paid. Christ concludes the parable by saying, "So my heavenly Father will do to every one of you if you do not forgive your brother or sister from your heart" (Mt 18:23-35).

It is impossible to miss the point. The kingdom of heaven exists wherever one person forgives another, and not superficially, but "from the heart." The kingdom of heaven is wherever mercy rules rather than vengeance.

Elsewhere in Saint Matthew's gospel Jesus compares the kingdom of heaven to a mustard seed. From the smallest of seeds springs up a shrub so big that "birds of the air come and make nests in its branches" (Mt 13:31-32). Then comes a similar image: the kingdom of heaven it is "like yeast that a woman took and mixed in with three measures of flour until all of it was leavened" (Mt 13:33).

A tiny seed, a small measure of yeast, a pinch of salt, a spark of light in the darkness–tiny things are capable of vast expansion and a transforming effect.

Jesus says the kingdom of heaven is like "a treasure hidden in a field," for which the joyful finder sells everything in order to own that field (Mt 13:44). Or it is like "a pearl of great value," for which one would sell everything else (Mt 13:45). The awareness of God's presence is "the buried treasure" and "the pearl of great price." We enter the kingdom of heaven when nothing is more important than the absolute beauty of God.

In another parable from Saint Matthew's gospel Jesus teaches that the "kingdom of heaven may be compared to someone who sowed good seeds in his field, but while everyone was asleep, an enemy came and sowed weeds among the wheat." The owner of the field orders his workers to leave the weeds alone so that they will not accidentally uproot any of the wheat, instructing them to wait until the harvest when they can separate the weeds out and burn them (Mt 13:24-30). Later he uses a similar metaphor–the kingdom of heaven is like "a net that was thrown into the sea and caught fish of every kind." Only after catching them are those worth keeping separated from those which are worthless (Mt 13:47-49). Both metaphors focus on God's patience, letting weeds grow with wheat in the field and gathering every sort of fish into the same net. We are living in the kingdom of God when we respect the lives of those around us, no matter what they are like.

Drawing on a range of simple images Jesus teaches his disciples that we enter the kingdom of heaven when we allow God's forgiveness, patience, and mercy to shape our response to others. The kingdom of heaven exists when we refuse to destroy or punish, leaving punishment to God at the Last Judgment.

In Saint Luke's gospel a group of Pharisees asks Jesus when the kingdom of God is coming. He responds, "The kingdom of

God is not coming with things that can be observed, nor will they say, 'Look, here it is!' or 'There it is!' For in fact the kingdom of God is among you" (Lk 17:20-21). Saint Paul says something similar in his letter to the Colossian church: "The Father has rescued us from the power of darkness and transferred us into the kingdom of his beloved Son" (Col 1:13). The kingdom of God is simply life in Christ–not a concept of Christ or trying to live according to principles we think of as Christian, but living in his presence, being aware of him in the things and people that surround us, no matter where we are. We understand that our obedience is to Christ and that all other demands made on our lives and resources are to be respected only if they are not in conflict with the commandments of Christ.

There is a story told by the poet Yevgeny Yevtushenko that gives us a glimpse of a sudden experience of the kingdom of heaven–in Russia, in the midst of war, with Stalin ruling from the Kremlin, and Hitler's armies pushing eastward.

In 1944 Yevtushenko's mother took him from Siberia to Moscow. They were in the huge crowd that witnessed a procession of twenty thousand German prisoners of war being marched across Red Square.

Yevtushenko recalls in his autobiography:

The pavements swarmed with onlookers, cordoned off by soldiers and police. The crowd was mostly women–Russian women with hands roughened by hard work, lips untouched by lipstick, and with thin hunched shoulders which had borne half of the burden of the war. Every one of them must have had a father or a husband, a brother or a son killed by the Germans. They gazed with hatred in the direction from which the column was to appear.

At last we saw it. The generals marched at the head, massive chins stuck out, lips folded disdainfully, their whole demeanor meant to show superiority over their plebeian victors. "They smell of perfume, the bastards," someone in the crowd said with hatred. The women were clenching their fists. The soldiers and policemen had all they could do to hold them back.

All at once something happened to them. They saw German soldiers, thin, unshaven, wearing dirty blood-stained bandages, hobbling on crutches or leaning on the shoulders of their comrades; the soldiers walked with their heads down. The street became dead silent—the only sound was the shuffling of boots and the thumping of crutches.

Then I saw an elderly woman in broken-down boots push herself forward and touch a policeman's shoulder, saying, "Let me through." There must have been something about her which made him step aside. She went up to the column, took from inside her coat something wrapped in a colored handkerchief and unfolded it. It was a crust of black bread. She pushed it awkwardly into the pocket of a soldier, so exhausted that he was tottering on his feet. And now from every side women were running toward the soldiers, pushing into their hands bread, cigarettes, whatever they had. The soldiers were no longer enemies. They were people.[12]

This is the sort of story most history books pass over—miraculous moments when enmity is replaced by mercy, compassion opens the way to actions of healing and forgiveness, and plain poverty becomes poverty of spirit. The gesture of a single old woman broke through what Saint Paul describes as "the dividing wall of enmity" (Eph 2:14). Her eyes had been opened to see suffering German boys rather than murderous Nazi soldiers. Her response was to give away what little she had, a carefully saved piece of black bread. Was she surprised afterward by what she had done and the flood of gifts others had made in the wake of her small gesture of love? It was a moment when the kingdom of heaven flooded across Red Square.

Blessed are they who mourn . . .

In the deserts of the heart,
Let the healing fountain start . . .
                    —W. H. Auden, "In Memory of W. B. Yeats"

When we die, we will not be criticized for having failed to work
miracles. We will not be accused of having failed to be theolo-
gians or contemplatives. But we will certainly have some expla-
nation to offer to God for not having mourned unceasingly.
                    —Saint John Climacus[13]

We could also say, "Blessed are they who grieve," or "Blessed
are they who weep." The word used in the Greek New Testament, *penthein*, signifies intimate, intense, heart-breaking sorrow.

Poverty of spirit is inseparable from mourning. Without poverty of spirit, I am always on guard to keep what I have for
myself, and to keep me for myself. An immediate consequence
of poverty of spirit is becoming sensitive to the pain and losses
of people around me, not only those whom I happen to know
and care for, but also people I don't know and don't want to
know. To the extent that I open my heart to others, I will do
whatever I can to help—pray, share what I have, even share
myself.

The most common grief is linked with death, the anguish of
a devastating loss, having to live without someone we still love,
desperately miss, and will never see again in this world.

Perhaps the worst grief is experienced by those people who
are so numbed by loss that they cannot cry. Their eyes feel like

desert sand. In such a state one prays for tears just as people living in a region of drought pray for rain. When tears come at last, we find ourselves inside a waterfall of God's grace. Part of being made in the image and likeness of God is being able to cry.

Twice in the gospels we are told of Jesus crying. The first occasion happened as he stood gazing at Jerusalem from a distance. "And when he drew near and saw the city, he wept over it" (Lk 19:41). It must have been a bewildering experience for his disciples. They saw a shining, golden-walled city dominated by its great Temple, with people like themselves streaming busily in and out of the fortified gateways. Jesus saw Jerusalem's destruction, the suffering of the city's inhabitants, and the enslavement and deportation of its survivors. He wept for the victims of a catastrophe decades in the future, but so real to him, so immediate, so devastating, that he grieved as if it were happening at that moment. He said to those who were with him, "Would that today you knew the things that make for peace!" (Lk 19:42).

The eleventh chapter of the gospel of Saint John records the occasion when Jesus made his way to the tomb in Bethany of his friend Lazarus, who had been dead four days. Before calling Lazarus back to life, he shared fully in the grief of Lazarus's sisters and friends. Verse 35 says simply, "Jesus wept." "There is no shorter verse in the Bible, nor is there a larger text," commented John Donne, the seventeenth-century poet and priest. It is one of those events when we see Jesus first as true man, responding to death with grief, and then as true God, reviving a corpse.

One could imagine in both cases a more intellectual, a more knowing, a more aloof response—like a scientist who knows what must happen if certain chemicals are mixed. Gazing at Jerusalem, Jesus could have told his disciples with academic detachment about the futility of violent resistance to imperial Rome and the disaster that would result for those who would seek salvation with the sword. Before summoning his dead friend Lazarus back to life, he could have chastised Lazarus's sisters, Mary and Martha, for their lack of faith. But the all-knowing Jesus is also a man of absolute compassion. Love is not detached or dry-eyed, satisfied that bad choices lead to tragic results or that mortal man is subject to mortal illness.

Jesus wept. But this is not simply a fact from the remote past. Because he is still with us, Jesus *weeps.* He rose from the dead, and with him rose his capacity to grieve. We find in his tears the sacrament of tears, the blessing that it is to mourn. We find his tears in our tears.

I think of friends of ours, Tom and Glinda Johnson-Medland, who for seven years prayed for a child and finally conceived one only to see her die before birth. "I became furious with God," Tom recalls, "and felt totally betrayed. If this was how God treated his friends . . . "

Fortunately, the priest Tom turned to in the midst of his rage and grief had good advice. "I don't care how angry you are at God," the priest said, "just get into church every week and take the mother of God some flowers. Stand in front of her icon, or kneel there, or roll around on the floor—I don't care. Scream, yell, cry, curse, I don't care, but go and be with her. She is the mother of our Lord, and she knows. She understands the loss of a child. Will you promise me you will do that? And take Glinda with you as often as she can go."

There was no false piety in the priest's advice, no glib slogans about God's inscrutable will or how happy they ought to be that their child was in heaven. Instead, he sent Tom and Glinda to Christ's mother, who herself was made a refugee by Herod, saw her Son condemned, saw nails hammered through his limbs, stood at the foot of the cross, and took part in his burial.

Tom kept his promise. Most of the time, laying flowers on the icon, he was in tears. "Tears gushed from deep in me. I was tapping into a sorrow I did not know, unleashing emotions I had never dreamed possible."

Glinda, herself a therapist, says that for months she often felt close to losing her sanity.

Tom and Glinda's grieving was long and painful, yet somehow the weekly gift of flowers to the mother of God helped them. "She became," Tom says, "our sweetness and our health, a meadow with softening flowers, our tears in the cleansing path of sorrow, our nurse in times of sickness, our mother when we needed to be held."

Looking back two years later, Glinda said that her experience taught her that "mourning creates transparency in people. It tells people that we are in pain and that we have experienced some type of loss. It opens us up for others to know. What we grieve over and mourn for reveals who we are. If we mourn our lack of money, it betrays our values. If we mourn child poverty, it exposes our heart."

Speaking as a therapist, she points to another lesson: "Mourning—the public expression of sorrow—helps us integrate our grief. The inability to mourn losses appropriately results in depression, psychosis, and physical illness. Until we can live with the reality of the loss of a loved one, the loss of a particular relationship, the loss of a piece of whom we once were, we have not integrated our grief. In a way, we are not living in reality."[14]

It is not only the death of people we love that causes mourning. The repentant woman who washed the feet of Christ with her tears was mourning the damage her actions had caused others and herself, bearers of God's image (Lk 7:38).

There are tears of the apostle Peter when the rooster crowed after his third denial of Christ. Hours before, Peter had nearly killed a man in his passion to defend his master. Since then he had been too afraid to admit he even knew him. Perhaps in Peter's denial there was also anger at God that this tragedy had been permitted. Then at last a flood of tears—for Christ's suffering, and for himself for having been a coward and a liar.

Anyone who has lived into adulthood has a large supply of memories that arouse shame and regret: lies told, times of cowardice, help not given, forgiveness refused, passions given free reign, harm caused others. There is a great deal in our lives for which we can only lament, do penance, and seek forgiveness.

One saint who symbolizes a life of mourning for past sins is Mary of Egypt, a woman of the fifth century. Explore any Orthodox church and probably you will find her icon—an emaciated, white-haired woman wearing little and standing among barren forms suggesting the desert. Each year during Lent, in every Orthodox parish, there is a public reading of the story of how Father Zosima, a monk who lived in the desert southeast of Jerusalem, one day caught sight of a human figure disappearing into the bushes. Pursuing the stranger, he heard her voice calling on him to turn his eyes away because she had no clothing. Father Zosima gave her his cloak, after which she spoke to him from a distance, telling him how, in Alexandria, she had abandoned herself to promiscuous pleasures and diversions. On a whim she joined a group of pilgrims going to Jerusalem, seducing some of them along the way. Then in Jerusalem she experienced a miracle. Looking at an icon of Christ's mother in a church courtyard, a simple image of self-giving love and purity, she was overwhelmed with remorse. Afterward she entered the church. Venerating a relic of the cross, she heard a voice telling her, "If you cross the Jordan, you will find peace." Taking these few words literally, for forty-seven years she lived a solitary life, praying day and night, fighting an invisible war with demons, surviving on plants and spring water. Father Zosima visited her a second time to bring her Communion. On his third visit, he discovered her dead body. She left a message in the sand to let him know she had died on the night of Christ's passion.

Mary of Egypt is one of those saints who sum up for many people "everything that is wrong with Christianity." Measured against modern definitions of sanity, Mary of Egypt is a lunatic. Her "unnecessary, church-instilled guilt" over alleged sins turned her into a masochist living in caves, nearly starving herself to death, and for what? A few wild years in her youth.

But for most of Christian history, saints such as Mary of Egypt were universally regarded as models of lucidity rather than madness. They represented the sanity of repentant mourning.

The tears they shed over their past sins restored the image of God in themselves. They had sinned on a grand scale, and then they repented on a similar scale. It wasn't that they imagined their sacrifices could purchase God's mercy; rather, they saw the ascetic life as a way of washing themselves clean in the presence of God.

Christianity, incarnational religion that it is, has always sought to do things in a way that holds body and soul together. The church therefore looks for ways to bring repentance not only into one's thoughts but into day-to-day physical activities. Repentance is not only regret in the mind but prayer and fasting, each reinforcing the other.

Raskolnikov, in Dostoevsky's *Crime and Punishment*, is a modern example of a man whose only hope is repentance. He had lost all sense of God and developed a philosophical justification for homicide: he convinced himself that certain people—the clever, the brilliant, the born leaders—are not subject to the same pedestrian moral code imposed on ordinary people. For people like himself, good can be achieved through evil means. After careful planning, he kills an old moneylender—and also an unexpected witness, an innocent, simpleminded girl who happens to be present. For some time afterward he feels no shame for what he did, even the slaying of the girl with the absolutely pure heart, but gradually the horror of his actions begins to dawn on him. He has the chance of not being found out—there is no evidence that proves his guilt, no witness to the crime, no trace of the axe. Yet finally he feels compelled to tell the truth and accept imprisonment and exile in Siberia in order to make a fresh beginning.

The investigator, Porfiry Petrovich, is among those who help Raskolnikov see the path that will lead to recovery. Petrovich even helps him see that, great though his sin was, it could have been worse. After all, his theory of justified murder cost only two lives: "If you had come up with a different theory [like a Napoleon], you might have done something a hundred million times more hideous." He goes on to assure Raskolnikov that "suffering is a good thing, after all. . . . No matter that you'll be passing into a different category of people [convict society]. You're not going to miss your comforts, are you, with a heart like yours? What matter if no one will see you for a long time? The point lies in you, not in time. Become a sun and everyone will see you."[15]

Finally comes the mourning that is not only for a dead family member or for the sins of one's own life, but grieving because we are among the children of Adam and Eve. Even the person who has never harmed a fly is implicated in murder simply by belonging to the human race.

In Dostoevsky's crowning work, *The Brothers Karamazov*, there is the Christlike monk, Father Zosima. Many people travel long distances in order to see him briefly, to seek a word of advice, an answer to a question that tortures them, an assurance of forgiveness. Close to death, Father Zosima tells his life story to his beloved young cell attendant, Alyosha Karamazov. He recalls that as a child, in a time of illness, God had entrusted him with a great truth, which he first expressed to his mother: "Each of us," he told her, "is guilty in everything before everyone, and I most of all." Of course she objects, telling her feverish son that, after all, he is no murderer or robber. The boy cannot explain or justify his truth, but assures her with even more conviction that "each of us is guilty before everyone, for everyone and everything."[16]

It is a useful spiritual exercise to consider the ways we are connected to each other and the implications of being so dependent on so many. The food I ate at my last meal involved the skills and labor of many people, not only those who grew it, packed it, transported it, and finally cooked and served it, but people down through the centuries who are part of the chain of discovery and tradition that is the history of agriculture and the craft of cooking. Bakers knead bread not only with their own hands but with the hands of those who taught them to bake. Few words in this book were coined in my lifetime. The tools of communication are all anonymous gifts.

We depend on each other: farmers, doctors, nurses, mechanics, plumbers, teachers, builders, printers, engineers, cooks, drivers, mail handlers, shopkeepers, mechanics, carpenters, paper makers, book binders . . . the list is as bulky as the Manhattan Yellow Pages. In fact, it is far bigger, because the Yellow Pages has to do only with the living, while we live from the accumulated knowledge, wisdom, and labor of every generation before us.

It is not only our physical well-being that depends on others. Our attitudes toward the world around us have in large measure been assimilated from family, friends, teachers, pastors, storytellers, film makers, politicians, journalists. Ways of response, directions taken in life—these too are shaped by many factors. Few wish to fight in wars, but many do so—because of social obligation, fear, propaganda, peer-group pressure. Through work, money, or politics, who beyond the age of infancy is not involved in the elaborate infrastructure of war?

The autonomous person doesn't exist. Even a hermit living in a cave on a cliff of Mount Athos is part of a community on which his life depends and in which his vocation of solitary prayer was shaped and remains rooted. At least once a week some younger monk will lower a basket of food down the cliff wall. The hermit appears to be alone, but his vocation is social—he is praying for us, often in tears.

Christ's tears as he gazed on Jerusalem were shed not for anything he had done or failed to do, but were tears of grief for *our* sins. His prayer was and is, "Would that today you knew the things that make for peace!"

God grant us the gift of tears: for those whom we miss, for our past sins, for the sins of others, for the violence we do to each other and to the world God gives to us each day. It is this condition of soul that Saint Paul wrote of in his letter to Timothy: "Christ Jesus came into the world to save sinners—of whom I am first" (1 Tm 1:15).

... for they shall be comforted.

The key word in Greek, *panakalein*, means not only "to be comforted or consoled" but "finding an ally or helper." It also signifies being invited to a banquet. *Panakalein* has still another meaning in classical Greek: "to exhort or encourage." In the plays of Aeschylus it was used to describe troops cheering each other on as they went into battle. For Aristotle, the verb meant exciting and energizing the mind. In this beatitude the word suggests the very opposite of a grudging pardon or conditional forgiveness.

This is forgiveness such as the father of the Prodigal Son showered on the son whom he feared he had lost forever. Having demanded and been given his share of the inheritance, the boy had left home and lived a wasteful life until he was reduced to attending pigs, as low a calling as a pork-abhorring Jew could imagine. Finally, finding himself living with hogs and sharing their food, he decided to go home, not expecting pardon—he realized he had forfeited all filial rights—but hoping his father might allow him to live among the servants. The father saw his repentant son in the distance, ran out to meet him, embraced him, kissed him, welcomed him home, replaced his rags with fine clothing, gave him a golden ring, and had a feast prepared, "for this son of mine was dead and is alive again. He was lost and is found" (Lk 15:24).

It's a complex drama. The boy had squandered a large part of the family fortune and, in a society in which the family unit was far stronger than it tends to be in our own, brought shame not only on himself but on his household. He had left behind a desolate father and, if she was still alive, a grieving mother, as well as a brother who may well have been glad the other had

46

left. One can hear the boy muttering "to hell with them all" as he slams the door on his way to "freedom." There was nothing the parents could do but pray for him.

Jesus gives few details about the son who fled from his home except to say he lived a dissolute life, wasting his inheritance. One can take the words literally and think of people we know who have done more or less the same thing. Better yet, we can find *ourselves* in the Prodigal Son, even if we haven't yet landed in the gutter. So much that we do is wasteful—time wasted, talents wasted, opportunities wasted.

We can also glimpse ourselves in the "good" brother who never left home and has lived by the rules. Far from sharing in his father's joy, he is furious, wishing his father would punish rather than welcome and forgive.

"Home" in the parable is a metaphor for the kingdom of God, which we are meant to receive but have fled from in every possible way, while the parable's father represents God the Father, who gives each of us various gifts—our "inheritance"—aware that some will leave home from time to time, but who remains ready to welcome us the moment we turn back toward our home, the kingdom of God. "Repentance" translates the Greek word *metanoia*, literally "turning around, doing an about-face." God's welcome is the consolation we receive by embracing repentance. The consolation given is like a banquet of joy: the discovery that the smallest repentant gesture on our part can open a flood of divine mercy.

Blessed are the meek...

O the magnitude of meekness!
  —Christopher Smart, "The Nativity of Our Lord and Savior"

The lion can be tamed and made obedient, but your own wrath renders you wilder than any lion.
  —Saint John Chrysostom[17]

Another rung of the ladder of the beatitudes—from poverty of spirit to mourning to meekness.

The Greek word translated as "meek," *praus*, was used to describe a wild animal who had been tamed and made gentle: a horse that would accept a rider, a dog that would tend sheep. In the human sphere it refers to a person who disciplines himself to be gentle rather than severe, nonviolent rather than violent. Aristotle saw meekness as the virtue that lies between opposing extremes of anger: cold cruelty, on the one hand, and burning wrath, on the other. The meek person is neither too hasty nor too slow-tempered; such a person bears reproaches and slights, is not bent on revenge, is free from bitterness and belligerence, possesses tranquility and steadiness of spirit.

For Jews, meekness is the essential quality of the human being in relationship to God. The equivalent Hebrew word, *anaw*, is often used in the psalms to describe the stance of a man or woman aligned with God. Such a person seeks God's guidance and is not bitter or resentful in obedience to the divine Law, though it is one of the glories of Judaism that the human being, however meek, is called to be more than God's "yes-man."

Ironically, the word *meek* was brought to England by Viking warriors; it has its roots in the Old Norse word for "soft"— *mjark*. *Meek* not only rhymes with *weak* but for many people indicates much the same thing, though its actual meaning has nothing to do with decrepitude or cowardice but with showing patience and humility, with gentleness.

While meekness is a hard virtue for everyone, men especially have fled from being labeled as meek. We have been made to think of meekness as a feminine quality: "Women are from Venus, men are from Mars," etc. For many, the male archetypes are cowboys, gun-slingers, and the Marlboro Man. Normally it isn't women who shoot first and ask questions later. "This is the Gospel According to John Wayne," says Father Joseph Donders, a Dutch priest who has spent most of his life in Africa. "No matter who plays the lead, the story is always the same. When faced by bad men, people evil right down to the marrow of their bones, the only solution is to kill them. It is a 'gospel' in the sense that it is the defining story for many people."

One of the synonyms of *meek, humble,* has also had bad press. In Charles Dickens's novel *David Copperfield* there is the spider-like character of Uriah Heap, a cunning and loveless figure who never tires of describing himself as "a humble man." Few aspire to humility; we prefer being proud. "I'm proud to be _____ (fill in the blank)." We're proud of who we are, what we've done, the national or ethnic group to which we happen to belong. Coming "from humble origins" means not being born with a silver spoon in your mouth but, through perseverance and hard work, leaving poverty behind and achieving things "to be proud of."

Understood biblically, meekness is making choices and exercising power with a divine rather than a social reference point. Meekness has nothing to do with blind obedience to the rulers in whatever country we happen to live in or to bosses in our work place or compliance with that still more powerful force, our peer group. Meek Christians do not allow themselves to be dragged along by the tides of political power or to be led by the smell of money. Such rudderless persons have cut themselves off from their own conscience, God's voice in their heart, and thrown away their God-given freedom. Meekness is an attribute of following Christ, whatever the risks.

The person who is meek toward God will have the strength not to commit or sanction evil deeds against a neighbor. True meekness provides the strength to disobey, no matter what the punishment.

Consider Abraham. Without meekness, there would be no Abraham, only a long-forgotten Abram, immobilized in his possessions and the details of his life, unable to leave Ur—a busy man dismissing strange voices that called him to wander off to unseen places. Yet this icon of meekness, at God's call, uprooted himself from his home, allowing himself and his family to be led he knew not where—only that he would be guided to a "land which I will show you" (Gn 12:1). Yet Abraham is not simply the Creator's "Amen chorus." Later in life, he passionately bargains with God in an effort to prevent the destruction of Sodom. Confronted with Abraham's appeal, God agrees to spare the city if fifty just men can be found among the inhabitants, and finally God assents to acquit the city even for the sake of ten just men. Sadly, there were not even ten upright citizens, and the depraved city was destroyed (Gn 18:23-33). But the book of Genesis preserves the remarkable story of meek Abraham and almighty God bargaining with each other just as merchants and customers still bargain throughout the markets of the Middle East.

The same meekness marks Abraham when there was conflict between his herdsmen and those of his nephew Lot. "Then Abram said to Lot, 'Let there be no strife between you and me, and between your herdsmen and my herdsmen, for we are kinsmen. Is not the whole land before you? Separate yourself from me. If you take the left hand, then I will go to the right; or if you take the right hand, then I will go to the left.' And Lot raised his eyes and saw that the Jordan valley was well watered

Icon of Mary

everywhere like the garden of the LORD, like the land of Egypt, in the direction of Zoar. . . . So Lot chose for himself all of the Jordan valley" (Gn 13:8-11). It was through meekness that the Promised Land itself was given to Abraham.

In psalm after psalm we are assured that God hears the cry of the humble, that God favors the lowly, that his judgment is in their favor rather than in favor of the proud and mighty. Psalm 25 says that God

> leads the humble in what is right
> and teaches the humble his ways.

In Psalm 149 God "adorns the humble"—not the mighty—"with victory," while in Isaiah the meek shall "obtain fresh joy in the LORD" (Is 29:19).

Iron-willed Moses, leader of the Jewish people in their forty-year sojourn in the Sinai Desert, was regarded as "meek above everyone on the face of the earth" (Nm 12:3). Day after day Moses struggled to understand God's will and to obey, guiding a people who often looked back with nostalgia on their days of slavery in Egypt. He was a leader of strength but without vanity.

There is radiant meekness in Mary's response to the Archangel Gabriel: "Here I am, the servant of the Lord: Let it be with me just as you have said" (Lk 1:38). God did not simply cause Mary to be pregnant and explain its meaning to her after the fact. It was Mary's free acceptance of God's will that allowed the Second Person of the Holy Trinity to take flesh in her body and become her son. In all its meekness, no other act in human history has had such significance. Through Mary, our Creator became one with us in the flesh. She gave birth to the Savior, nourished him, cared for him, raised him, and accompanied him as a disciple.

Meekness is one of the principal attributes of Jesus Christ. He who calls the universe into being, who walks on water and brings the dead back to life, says of himself, "I am meek and humble of heart" (Mt 11:29).

Again and again in the gospels we see what meekness is.

Jesus was born in poverty in a cave meant to shelter animals. As a child he was a refugee in Egypt. Having reached adulthood, he owned nothing more than his clothing, not even having change in his pocket (answering a question about payment of taxes, he had to borrow a coin to show that Caesar's image was stamped upon it). He was one of the homeless: "The foxes have holes and the birds of the air have nests, but the Son of Man has nowhere to lay his head" (Mt 8:20).

Christ's first miracle—changing water into wine at the wedding in Cana—was done reluctantly, in meek submission to his mother's appeal, after telling her that it wasn't yet his time.

He often allows others to set the agenda. It is rare for Jesus to heal a person who hasn't sought his help. (Two exceptions are the man born blind and the man whom Peter wounded at the time Jesus was arrested.)

His messianic entry into Jerusalem was on the back of a borrowed donkey. A ruler of the ancient world would make his triumphal entrance into a city on horseback, and not just any horse but one fit for a ruler, reserved for him alone, and known by name. The donkey is a patient and gentle creature, the perfect symbol for a ruler who had rejected weapons and armies.

The night of the Last Supper, Christ provided the apostles—men who would become the first bishops—with an example of meek service to others: "He poured water into a basin and began to wash the disciples' feet" (Jn 13:5). It was an embarrassing action—Peter initially resisted. But in what better way could the Savior teach them the nature of love and what it means to serve rather than to rule? No Caesar ever washed anyone's feet. Christ's gesture reveals a degree of love and humility that none of us can ever fully comprehend.

Praying in the Garden of Gethsemane later that night, he pleaded with his Father, "If it is possible, take this cup from me," then added, "yet not what I want but what you want" (Mt 26:39). It is the prayer at the heart of the beatitude of meekness: to live God's will rather than our own.

Finally, we see the meekness of Christ bearing the cross and submitting to crucifixion, begging from the cross the forgiveness of his Father for those responsible for his death. "Father, forgive them for they know not what they are doing" (Lk 23:34).

One finds hundreds of stories of meekness in the teachings of the early monastic movement in Egypt and other desert places.

Abba Moses the Black, a former robber turned monk, was asked to join a meeting at which one brother was to be condemned for some sin or shortcoming, but Abba Moses failed to appear. Finally a priest was sent with the message, "Come, the community is waiting for you." Reluctantly Abba Moses came, but not before filling a cracked jug with water and carrying it with him. "Father, what does this mean?" he was asked as he reached the meeting place. "It is my sins flowing out behind me but I do not notice them. Thus I come to judge the sins of another." His meek gesture inspired the others to forgive rather than to condemn.[18]

Another Egyptian elder, Abba Anastasius, possessed a Bible, the whole of the Old and New Testaments, a rare treasure in the ancient world, but it was stolen from his cell. The thief took it to a dealer in manuscripts in Alexandria who looked through the many sheets of parchment but could not decide what to offer and so asked for some days to consider. Realizing he needed expert advice, he took the Bible to Abba Anastasius. The elder looked through the Bible as if he had never seen it before. "Do you think sixteen pieces of gold is a fair price?" the merchant asked. "Yes, it is a fine book. It is worth that price." Back in Alexandria the merchant met the man who had brought him the Bible, offering him sixteen piece of gold, and telling him of his visit to Abba Anastasius and his agreement about the price. "And did he say nothing more?" "No, that was all." "Well," said the thief, "I have changed my mind." He took back the Bible, hurried back to the monastery, not only returning the Bible but becoming a disciple of meek Abba Anastasius.[19]

Then there is the tale of Abba Macarius, who one day was returning from the marsh to his cell carrying palm leaves when he met the devil on the road. The devil attacked him repeatedly but in vain. Finally the devil asked, "What is your power, Macarius, that makes me powerless against you? All that you do, I do too. You fast, but I never eat. You keep vigil, but I never sleep. In one thing only do you beat me." Abba Macarius asked what that was. The devil said, "Your humility. Because of that I can do nothing against you."[20]

When I search my memory for models of meekness who have had a significant impact in the modern world, I think of people I met while writing about religious life in Russia in the Soviet era. They often spoke of the special role played in their lives by grandparents—men and women who continued coming to church and participating in the liturgy when every social pressure was mobilized to keep people away from church. Usually it was the grandmother who arranged the baptisms of her grandchildren. Those who remained active in church were meek but powerful, possessing inner strength. Neither the promise of reward nor the threat of punishment moved them. Every candle lit in church was an act of quiet resistance to an atheist state.

I remember Father Nicholas Preobrashenski, a priest I met in 1987 in Leningrad, as St. Petersburg was then called. Before entering the seminary, he had been a nuclear physicist. "Had things gone a little differently in my life," he told me, "I would probably be making nuclear weapons now!" We talked about the influences in his life that had led him toward Christian faith.

Born in 1944 in Pskov, he came from an Orthodox family. But as a boy he had stopped going to church or identifying with religion in any way. "I tried to hide every trace of belief. I was ashamed to show it, to witness it, before students and teachers. If you wore a cross, they would say, 'Ah, so you're a priest!' It was a very hard time for believers. We didn't know what was coming. A lot of churches were closed. So I learned to give the answers they wanted to hear, to say whatever was on television or in the papers."

His sister had died in the siege of Leningrad, and his father, born in 1915, had been in prison during part of the Stalin years, before the war. "Yet my father never lost his Christian view. 'Receive life as it comes to you,' he always told us, 'and never hold anyone to blame but yourself.' Father knew those who were responsible for his arrest, but he never spoke of them with anger."

As a teenager Father Nicholas had concentrated on science and eventually enrolled in the physics faculty at the university, where in time he became an expert in the separation of isotopes. "Then I began to specialize in military applications at the institute where I was working. At this time I also had a few papers accepted for publication. I was married, a father. It was the beginning of success in my life, really, but I felt something was missing and was drawn toward the church."

I asked him how that happened. "In the church I felt at home. I remember one day walking past one of the few churches in Leningrad that had not been closed. The door was open, a service was in progress, and I could smell incense. It was as if my parents and grandparents were in the incense. It was as if they took me by the hand and led me inside the church."

There were many further steps along the way—the interest his bishop took in him, the books brought to him by his father and uncle. "Study is important, but finally I am the sort of person who has to look at everything through my heart. I like to feel and not only to know. Step by step, I turned toward another side. Then, in 1978, after nine years in physics, I gave up my job at the institute and entered the seminary. But if it had not been for my family, I would not have taken the first step. Thank God, my wife was able to take the same steps with me. No one in my family ever tried to force me or argue me into belief, but I could always see in them what it meant to be Christian."

One sees a similar meekness in American women like Rosa Parks. Mrs. Parks was active in a black church in Montgomery, Alabama, and had been the local secretary of the National Association for the Advancement of Colored People. In 1955 she was working as a seamstress in a Montgomery department store. On December 1, at the end of her workday and after doing her grocery shopping, she boarded a public bus.

"When I got on the bus," she relates, "I noticed the Negro section in the back of the bus was filled. But there was one vacant seat in the middle section, the part we could use as long as no white people wanted the seats. On the third stop a few white people boarded the bus and they took all the designated white seats. There was one white man left standing. The driver turned around and said he needed those front seats so this white man could take a seat, which meant the ones we [four black people] were sitting on. The four of us would have to stand up in order to accommodate this one white passenger. This was segregation. When the driver first spoke, none of us moved. But then he spoke a second time with what I would call a threat. He said, 'You all better make it light on yourselves and let me have those seats.' At that point the other three stood up. The driver looked at me and asked me if I was going to stand up. I told him no, I wasn't. He said, 'If you don't stand up, I'm going to have you arrested.' I told him to go on and have me arrested. I was too tired to stand. I didn't exchange any more words with him."

Rosa Parks was arrested and spent the night in jail. "I wasn't happy at all," she remembers, "but I don't recall being extremely frightened. I just felt very much annoyed and inconvenienced because I had hoped to go home and cook supper and do whatever I had to do for the evening."[21]

That night forty black pastors, among them the recently ordained Martin Luther King Jr., met together and decided the time had come to try to end segregation on the city's bus system. King, the youngest minister in the group, was elected to head a group the pastors christened the Montgomery Improvement Association. In the year that followed, the black citizens of Montgomery refused to ride segregated buses, instead walking many thousands of miles, enduring not only inconvenience and exhaustion, but threats, taunts, violence, and bombings. Their long walk ended only when the Supreme Court ruled that racial segregation in public transportation violated the Constitution, overturning a Montgomery court's conviction of Rosa Parks. It was a major blow to structures of segregation everywhere in the United States.

The civil-rights movement that was born in America in 1955 was sparked by the meek gesture of a tired but determined Christian lady who said "no" to a bus driver.

As it happens, this chapter is being written during Lent. There is a prayer that Orthodox Christians use on a daily basis during the weeks of fasting that precede Easter, the prayer of Saint Ephraim the Syrian. It is an urgent appeal to God for meekness with all its qualities:

O Lord and Master of my life, take from me the spirit of sloth, faint-heartedness, lust for power and idle talk, but give to me, your servant, the spirit of chastity, humility, patience and love. O Lord and King, grant to me to see my own faults and not to judge my brother. For blessed art thou unto the ages of ages. Amen.

... for they shall inherit the earth.

You who wish to possess the earth now, take care. If you are meek, you will possess it; if ruthless, the earth will possess you.
—SAINT AUGUSTINE[22]

We are treated as . . . having nothing, and yet possess all things.
—SAINT PAUL (2 COR 6:8-10)

Christ promises each righteous person what he or she longs for—comfort to those who mourn, satisfaction to those who hunger and thirst for righteousness. The meek are promised a place on which to rest their feet.

This beatitude was already familiar to the Jews. They knew it from Psalm 37:

> Yet a little while longer and the wicked shall be no
>   more.
>   Though you search carefully for their place,
>   they will not be there.
>   But the meek shall inherit the earth
>   and rejoice in abundant prosperity.

The promise is echoed in psalm after psalm.

Inheritance as understood in law courts has to do with the distribution of property to the living after someone has died, but in a biblical context it means receiving all that God has promised. What God promises belongs to the heirs of God's promise, heirs not by birth but by choice, love, and obedience (the root meaning of which is "hearing").

It is easy to see that the meek own very little of this world's property. In fact, few people have owned less than Jesus Christ. But there is another way of seeing the world that sweeps away all certificates of ownership. It's an attitude suggested in a haiku by the Japanese poet, Issa, who was himself poor as a church mouse:

> The thief left it behind:
> the moon at the window.

A burglar can strip your house of everything and even burn it to the ground. But a burglar cannot steal the moon—or your honesty or decency or capacity to love. A thief cannot deprive you of your faith or make you like himself.

Some of Russia's meek were very like Issa in their attitude toward possessions. Putting on a pilgrim's garment that had no pockets, they left everything to pray their way from place to place, living on the bread others gave them. Owners of nothing, the least powerful people in the world, they found themselves the owners of an endless estate—roads, forests, churches, monasteries, places of pilgrimage—and guests of many kind people for whom it was a blessing to receive ambassadors of God.

There is also the witness of the primitive monastic movement—all those men and women fleeing a world officially Christianized in order to live in the deserts, places no one wanted or would shed blood to own. They "inherited" a land that others regarded with fear.

What do the meek long for? "A small domain on which to live quiet and peaceful lives," my friend Renée Zitzloff, mother of six, suggests. "A small plot of earth where their children can run and play and where they might grow vegetables, herbs and flowers, where they can lead godly lives and pass on that legacy to their children. For this they need earth, and God grants it to them. It is the same gift he gave Adam and Eve, but they lost it to Satan when they were cast out of Eden. With Christ's coming, he once again grants the earth to the meek so that they may re-create Eden."

"Life is so desperately physical!" my wife remarked this Lent as the fast took hold. Christ speaks about land, not clouds or rainbows. Christianity, like the Judaism that is its mother, takes material things seriously. The kingdom Christ promises is not an ethereal paradise of winged beings who have made themselves at home in the upper atmosphere; it is people raised body and soul from death—as we are and yet changed. The gospels provide only glimpses of what that transformation means—we are also given the image of the wedding feast—but one of the glimpses is this beatitude with its promise of land to the meek.

"The meek man is thought to lose everything," observed Saint John Chrysostom, a church Father of the fourth century, "but Christ promises the contrary, saying, 'No, it is the meek—he who is not rash nor boastful—who possesses his goods in safety, while the unsubdued person shall often lose his all and even lose his life.'"[23]

Blessed are they who hunger and thirst for righteousness...

Then the righteous will shine like the sun in the kingdom of their Father. He who has ears, let him hear.

—Jesus Christ (Mt 13:43)

Bread for myself is a physical question; bread for my neighbor is a spiritual question.

—Nikolai Berdyaev

Abba Joseph came to Abba Lot and said to him: "Father, according to my strength I keep a moderate rule of prayer and fasting, quiet and meditation, and as far as I can I control my imagination; what more must I do?" And the old man rose and held his hands toward the sky so that his fingers became like flames of fire and he said: "If you will, you shall become all flame."

—The Sayings of the Desert Fathers[24]

Another rung: from poverty of spirit to mourning to meekness and now to hungering and thirsting for righteousness.

Righteousness comes from the Old English word *rihtwis,* joining together "right" (morally pure) and "wise" (a method or manner of doing). A righteous person is a right-living person, living a moral, blameless life, right with both God and neighbor. The word in the Greek New Testament is *dikaoisune,* which means "righteousness, justice, the state of being justified." Each meaning has its place in understanding this beatitude.

"Feeding the Hungry" by the Master of Alkmaar

Righteousness suggests a life armed with virtues (from the Latin word for strength, *virtus*). To be lacking in virtue is to be powerless. It's like living in Kansas and having no storm cellar in which to take shelter when tornadoes are raking the land. The cultivation of virtues is the struggle to equip oneself to withstand attack—not of tornadoes but of temptations, including the temptation to be passive and to look the other way.

Jesus Christ doesn't say "Blessed are those who hope for righteousness," or "Blessed are those who campaign for righteousness," but "Blessed are they who *hunger and thirst* for righteousness"—that is, people who want what is right as urgently as a person in the desert wants a glass of water or a child in a refugee camp cries desperately for a crust of bread.

Hunger was a familiar experience to those who first heard the sermon on the mount; poverty was normal then, as it still is in much of the world. Those who had to cross the Negev Desert or the wilderness of Sinai would have vivid memories of wanting nothing so desperately as a mouthful of water.

If few readers of this book have themselves been threatened with starvation, still everyone from infancy onward has known hunger and thirst. It is a rare Sunday in our parish when we don't hear the sudden cries of a child desperate to nurse. Later on in life we encounter other appetites that are just as pressing but harder to satisfy—hunger for status, achievement, recognition, possessions, sexual hunger. But hungering for righteousness is unusual—possibly a rarer craving today in our world than it was in the days of the apostles.

In his sermons on the gospel of Saint Matthew, Saint John Chrysostom asks: "What sort of righteousness? He means either the whole of virtue, or that particular virtue which is opposed to covetousness."[25]

Covetousness is the driving force in many lives. How many times have I been miserable at not having something I urgently wanted, but the moment of possession only opens the door to the next urgent need—a soul-destroying cycle in which there is no such thing as enough. The hunger for righteousness is the one appetite that Christ blesses—not to covet possessions or achievement or recognition, but to live, through every action and perception, the kingdom of God.

Saint Leo the Great, bishop of Rome in the fifth century, has a similar stress in his homily on the beatitudes: "It is nothing bodily, nothing earthly, that this hunger, this thirst seeks for, but it desires to be satiated with the good food of righteousness and wants to be admitted to all the deepest mysteries, and be filled with the Lord Himself."[26] It is notable that Saint Leo, one of only three popes to be recognized as a doctor of the church, laid great stress on almsgiving and other social aspects of Christian life, for Christian life is less our ideas about God than how we live with those around us. To follow Christ and turn a blind eye toward the poor is a contradiction in terms.

There are so many unworthy appetites that can rule our lives. In *The Picture of Dorian Gray* Oscar Wilde describes a man ravenously hungry for youth and beauty. In this modern retelling of the legend of Doctor Faustus, a satanic bargain is struck so that a man's painted image ages instead of his body. The arrangement brings Dorian Gray no real joy, however, but only a sense of superiority and contempt toward others. From time to time he visits the painting hidden in his attic to see himself not as he appears in a mirror or in the eyes of others, but as he really is. What was once an image of youthful beauty finally becomes the portrait of a loathsome monster. The story ends in suicide committed before the portrait's revelation of who Gray has become. Wilde's moral is classic: we have to take charge of our hungers and thirsts or they take possession of us. Every uncontrolled passion or addiction is disfiguring.

In Victor Hugo's novel *Les Misérables* the pivotal event is a desperate man's theft of a loaf of bread in order to prevent his sister's children from starving to death. The culprit, Jean Valjean, is a good and honest man who cannot find work. He is struggling to survive in a society better organized to punish than to help; the social order is personified in the relentless and heartless Inspector Javert. There are several kinds of hunger at the foundation of the story: the urgent physical hunger of children in a world hostile to the poor; the loving hunger of Jean Valjean for the lives and well-being of his nieces and nephews; and finally, the author's prophetic hunger for a compassionate social order, a society in which no one is driven to theft in order to prevent the starvation of those who are defenseless. Truly, Victor Hugo hungered and thirsted for righteousness.

Christ calls on *us* to hunger for righteousness.

The first man in the Bible to be identified as righteous was Noah the ark-builder: "Noah was a righteous man, blameless in his generation; Noah walked with God" (Gn 6:9). The author of this section of Genesis says that, apart from Noah and his family, the rest of the human race made God regret having brought humankind into existence. Noah must have been the laughingstock of his neighbors, for who could appear more foolish than a man building a ship far from water while collecting pairs of animals and birds to put on board? Noah, the first zookeeper. Clearly, Noah, with his ear tilted toward a voice no one else heard, had bats in his bell tower. Yet it was his act of obedience to the Creator, in the face of his neighbors' jeers, that gave the human race and the animal kingdom a second chance. Thus he is the first *tsadik*–the first righteous man. According to Jewish tradition it is the *tsadik*, often perceived as a fool, who in each generation plays the role of Noah.

Was there really a Noah? Did he really build an ark? Perhaps Noah is only an inspired invention of a storytelling grandmother responding to a child's question about a sea shell found where there is no sea. I can almost hear her voice as she looks at the beautiful object her grandchild has given her: "Where there are sea shells, there must have been an ocean, and therefore a time when the whole world was submerged, and, if so, it was the work of God. If we could listen well enough to this shell, it would tell a story of God's justice and mercy and how even one faithful person–a single *tsadik*–can save the world."

There may be reason to doubt there was a historical Noah, but the next righteous man in the Bible, the next *tsadik*, seems as real as my grandfather. Abraham too had his ears turned toward heaven. Responding to the divine command, he led his family, servants, and livestock away from Ur without knowing where God was leading them or what the purpose of their uprooting was.

The book of Psalms is full of the words *righteous* and *righteousness*. In Psalm 37 the righteous person, even though poor, is recognized as having the real wealth:

> Better is the little that the righteous person has
> than the abundance of many wicked. (Ps 37:16)

Psalm 92 compares those who are righteous to deeply rooted trees:

> The righteous flourish like the palm tree
> and grow like a cedar in Lebanon. (Ps 92:12)

In Psalm 119 righteousness is seen as a quality of God revealed in the divine law:

> I will praise you with an upright heart
> when I learn your righteous ordinances.
> (Ps 119:7)

> The sum of your word is truth;
> and every one of your righteous ordinances
> endures forever. (Ps 119:160)

The book of Proverbs is even more crowded with verses about righteousness and its qualities. A righteous person is someone who is unflinchingly truthful.

> All the words of my mouth are righteous;
> there is nothing twisted or crooked in them.
> (Prv 8:8)

The righteous are never a threat to their neighbors:

> With their mouths the godless would destroy their
> neighbors,
> but by knowledge the righteous are delivered.
> (Prv 11:9)

The righteous do not depend on or covet possessions:

> Those who trust in their riches will wither,
> but the righteous will flourish like green leaves.
> (Prv 11:28)

The righteous are just not only to humans but to animals:

> The righteous know the needs of their animals,
> but the mercy of the wicked is cruel. (Prv 12:10)

The righteous are eager to share:

> All day long the wicked covet,
> but the righteous give and do not hold back.
> (Prv 21:26)

The righteous are brave in the face of danger:

> The wicked flee when no one pursues,
> but the righteous are as bold as a lion.
> (Prv 28:1)

The righteous safeguard the poor:

> The righteous know the rights of the poor;
> the wicked have no such understanding.
> (Prv 29:7)

The prophet Isaiah identifies the righteous person as the messiah to come:

He shall see the fruit of the travail of his soul and
     be satisfied;
   by his knowledge shall the righteous one, my
        servant, make many to be accounted
        righteous;
   and he shall bear their iniquities. (Is 53:11)

Jeremiah has a similar vision:

Behold, the days are coming . . . when I will raise up for
David a righteous branch, and he shall reign as king and
deal wisely, and shall execute justice and righteousness in
the land. (Jer 23:5)

Christ warns us that it is the righteous who are saved at the
Last Judgment:

Then the righteous will answer him, "Lord, when did we
see you hungry and feed you, or thirsty and give you
drink?" . . . . And they [who were not merciful to the least
person] will go away into eternal punishment, but the righteous into eternal life. (Mt 25:37, 46)

The righteous person is someone in whom others, especially
those in need, experience the mercy of God.

   In many bookshops this book will be placed in the section
labeled "spirituality," a good word that means living in the Holy
Spirit. These days, though, it often suggests that by adopting
the right method of prayer or meditation you will be lifted above
the world, its distracting problems and hopeless suffering and
enter into the bliss of God (or Buddha or a Hindu deity). Christian spirituality has nothing to do with losing contact with those
who suffer.

   A Christian is obliged to see and respond to the real world with
all its fear, pain, and bloodstains, to be a rescuer, to protect the
defenseless, to participate here and now in God's righteousness. A

way of prayer that makes one blind to the least person is a door to hell. William Blake wrote:

> The beggar's rags, fluttering in the air
> does to rags the heavens tear.[27]

The elders of the desert again and again give us examples of righteousness.

Abba Theodore of Pherme, following the advice of Abba Macarius, sold his only possessions of value, three books, and gave the money to the poor. Abba Macarius on one occasion helped a thief rob Macarius's own dwelling. All such gestures communicate self-emptying love, *kenosis* in Greek. Dying to one's possessions, refusing to condemn, causes light to shine in the darkness.

Abba Lot said to Abba Joseph, "If you will, you shall become all flame." Hungering and thirsting for righteousness is the beatitude of fire, the overwhelming longing that life should be on earth as it is in heaven.

The Orthodox nun Mother Maria Skobtsova is one of those who became all flame.

She was born in 1891 into an aristocratic family in Riga, Latvia, in those days part of Russia. In her youth she wrote poetry; one of her works, *Scythian Shards*, was well known in St. Petersburg's literary circles. In the period of impending revolution she joined the Socialist Revolutionary Party, but when the Bolsheviks overthrew the democratic government in October 1917, she left for Anapa on the Black Sea coast. There she married an anti-Bolshevik officer, bore two children, and also served as mayor, in the process facing abuse from both the left and the right. Then, in 1923, threatened with assassination, she joined the throng of refugees uprooted by revolution and civil war and made her way to France.

In Paris her second child soon died of meningitis, a tragedy that initiated a profound conversion. She emerged from her mourning with a determination to seek "a more authentic and purified life." She felt she saw a "new road before me and a new meaning in life . . . to be a mother for all, for all who need maternal care, assistance, or protection." Immersing herself in efforts to assist destitute Russian refugees, she sought them out in prisons, hospitals, mental asylums, and in the slums. Increasingly she emphasized the religious dimension of this work, the insight that "each person is the very icon of God incarnate in the world." With this recognition came the need "to accept this awesome revelation of God unconditionally, to venerate the image of God" in her brothers and sisters.

Her bishop urged her to become a nun after her marriage ended, but she took the step only with his assurance that she would be free to develop a new type of monasticism, engaged in the world and marked by the "complete absence of even the subtlest barrier which might separate the heart from the world and its wounds."

In 1932 she made her monastic profession and became Mother Maria. Rejecting monastic enclosure, she leased a house in Paris with space enough for a chapel, a soup kitchen, and a shelter for destitute refugees. Giving herself the least, her "cell" was a cot in the basement beside the boiler.

Her house became a center not only for the works of mercy but for dialogue. While her kitchen was crowded with the "down and out," the drawing room—and in the summer, the backyard—became a place where leading émigré intellectuals of Paris debated the relation between faith and the social questions of the day. Out of their discussions a new movement was born, Orthodox Action, committed to realizing the social implications of the gospel. "The meaning of the liturgy must be translated into life," said Mother Maria. "It is why Christ came into the world and why he gave us our liturgy."

The final act of Mother Maria's life began with the German occupation of Paris in 1940. In the context of Nazi racism, her commitment to seek out and revere each person as an icon of God assumed a deliberately subversive significance. Aside from "normal" hospitality to the poor, she, her chaplain, Father

Dimitri Klepinin, and her son, Yuri, did all that was in their power to assist Jews and others being sought by the Nazis. During the fearful days of July 1942, when thousands of Jews were rounded up in the Velodrome d'Hiver, Mother Maria succeeded in penetrating the sports stadium and, assisted by garbage collectors, smuggled out Jewish children in garbage bins. That same month, when an edict was published requiring Jews to wear the yellow star, she wrote a poem entitled "Israel":

> Two triangles, a star,
> The shield of King David, our forefather.
> This is election, not offense.
> The great path and not an evil.
> Once more in a term fulfilled,
> Once more roars the trumpet of the end;
> And the fate of a great people
> Once more is by the prophet proclaimed.
> Thou art persecuted again, O Israel,
> But what can human malice mean to thee,
> Who have heard the thunder from Sinai?

Though aware she was under Gestapo surveillance, Mother Maria continued her work in behalf of Jews. To give up was out of the question, she told friends. A diary entry from that period of her life reveals the fidelity God had given her: "There is one moment when you start burning with love and you have the inner desire to throw yourself at the feet of some other human being. This one moment is enough. Immediately you know that instead of losing your life, it is being given back to you twofold."

On February 8, 1943, she and Father Dimitri were arrested. She readily admitted the charge of helping Jews elude police roundups–it was nothing more than her Christian duty.

When Father Dimitri was brought in for interrogation, the Gestapo agent, a man named Hoffman, decided at first on a conciliatory approach. It backfired, as the following dialogue testifies:

Hoffman:	If we release you, will you promise never again to aid Jews?
Father Dimitri:	I can say no such thing. I am a Christian and must act as I must. *(Hoffman struck Father Dimitri across the face.)*
Hoffman:	Jew lover! How dare you talk of helping those swine as being a Christian duty! *(Father Dimitri, recovering his balance, held up the cross from his cassock.)*
Father Dimitri:	Do you know *this* Jew? *(For this, Father Dimitri was knocked to the floor.)*

He, Mother Maria, and her son, Yuri, were taken to Compiègne, where Father Dimitri managed to serve the liturgy each day and to begin preparing Yuri for ordination.

In his last letter from Compiègne to friends in Paris, later found in a suitcase returned to his home, Yuri wrote, "I am absolutely calm, even somewhat proud to share Mama's fate. I promise you I will bear everything with dignity. Whatever happens, sooner or later we shall all be together. I can say in all honesty that I am not afraid of anything any longer. . . . I ask anyone whom I have hurt in any way to forgive me. Christ be with you!" In December, Father Dimitri and Yuri were transferred to Buchenwald, where both died that winter. Yuri was twenty-four.

Sent to the notorious Ravensbrück women's concentration camp north of Berlin, Mother Maria managed to survive almost to the war's end, all the while caring for the bodies and souls of her fellow prisoners. She occasionally traded bread for needle and thread in order to embroider images that gave her strength. Her last work of art was an embroidered icon of Mary, the mother of God, holding the child Jesus, his hands and feet already bearing the wounds of the cross.

On Good Friday, March 31, 1945, with the gunfire of approaching Russian troops audible in the distance, Mother Maria took the place of a Jewish prisoner who was to be sent to the gas chamber and died in her place.

"At the Last Judgment I shall not be asked whether I was successful in my ascetic exercises, nor how many bows and prostrations I made," she had explained earlier in her life. "Instead I shall be asked, Did I feed the hungry, clothe the naked, visit the sick and the prisoners? That is all I shall be asked."[28]

... for they shall be satisfied.

I have come that they might have life, and have it abundantly.
                                        –JESUS CHRIST (JN 10:10)

A verse from Psalm 22 is often used in Orthodox homes as a blessing at mealtime:

> The poor shall eat and be satisfied;
>   those who seek the LORD shall praise him.
> Their hearts will live forever. (v. 26)

We had a guest once who, after the blessing, said, "You've got to be kidding. Not even the rich are satisfied, yet you have a prayer about the poor being satisfied."

The psalm only makes sense if we understand that what is meant is not poverty only as an economic condition but poverty of spirit. Those who are not only poor but poor of spirit are grateful even though very little comes their way.

Metropolitan Anthony Bloom, who started life as a Russian refugee and seems likely to end it in London where he heads the Russian Orthodox diocese in Britain, was asked not long ago how a person might become humble. "It is too much to ask for," he replied. "Just try to be grateful."

We are not rewarded with cash prizes for being faithful. Righteousness can never be weighed on a grocer's scale. Physical hunger isn't an unusual condition in our world, nor is there any evidence that being a Christian improves one's diet. Most Christians are poor, and poverty is often a synonym for hunger.

In the beatitudes Christ teaches us to focus our hunger not on food and possessions but on righteousness: a life in unity with God, a life of mercy, a life transformed by love. This has nothing to do with disdain for life's material needs. Not a single crumb was wasted by prisoners in the Ravensbrück concentration camp, many of whose inmates died of diseases brought on by chronic malnutrition. Mother Maria treasured each crust of bread—but it was not bread she lived for.

We know the poor are often hungry and that many starve. On the other hand, are the rich filled? Saint Leo the Great wrote sixteen centuries ago:

> It is commonly thought that it is the rich who are made full because of their greed. No, Christ teaches, it is just the opposite. We are satisfied only from righteousness. So long as you live righteously, have no fear of poverty, do not tremble before hunger. The greedy are the very persons who lose everything, just as the one who is in love with righteousness possesses the goods of all men in safety.

In the early seventies *The New Yorker* printed an essay that had the intriguing title, "An Inquiry into Enoughness." The person who feels he or she has enough, it turned out, is hard to find. There is no such thing as enough. It seems to be the nature of emperors to covet larger empires. Robert Coles came away with similar conclusions when he wrote *Privileged Ones*, a book about the children of the affluent, many of whom have such fleeting glimpses of their busy parents that they often feel like wealthy orphans.

As part of the Catholic Worker community in New York City's Lower East Side, I occasionally met people who had practically nothing, in some cases not even a room of their own, yet they seemed to own Manhattan and to be bearers of treasure chests of wisdom. One of them was Charlie O'Keefe. Pink faced and with twinkling eyes, he was a down-but-not-out Jack Lemmon. Charlie had a weakness for the bottle, which meant that from time to time he disappeared from sight. The works of Shakespeare were on the tip of Charlie's tongue. He claimed ownership of the New York City Public Library as well as a derelict pier on the East River. Ladling soup for those who dined gratis at Saint Joseph's House, he might recite *Romeo and Juliet* one day, *Hamlet* the next, and *The Taming of the Shrew* the day after that. It was a great moment in his life, and mine, when we got him a pair of shoes that properly fit his large feet. I had imagined he hobbled because of some injury years before. He never mentioned that his shoes were too small. It was only because one shoe had split down the back that it dawned on us to look for a bigger pair in the community's clothing room. When we found nothing the right size, a friend and I took him to a local shoe shop and bought him a brand new pair. Charlie just about tap danced back to the soup kitchen.

Saint Joseph's House at that time was on Chrystie Street—a crumbling three-storey brick building that had been put up cheaply in the nineteenth century. The inside walls had been painted white when the Catholic Worker community took possession: the perfect color for appropriate graffiti. On the third floor, the office, various sayings from the church Fathers had been written here and there, but the text I think about most often was a line from the French poet Leon Bloy: "Joy is the most infallible sign of the presence of God."

Dorothy Day, the founder of the Catholic Worker, had come to live in the slums not because she felt obliged by God to immerse herself in ugliness but because of the beauty she found in places of poverty and the joy it often gave her: the beauty in faces, the beauty of trees and plants that managed to survive despite urban desolation, the beauty of kitchen smells at supper time coming from neighborhood apartments, the beauty of the liturgy even in the poorest parish church. She often quoted Dostoevsky's words: "The world will be saved by beauty."

Absolute Beauty, the beauty at the heart of beauty: Christ.

Blessed are the merciful...

We hand folks over to God's mercy, and show none ourselves.
                                    —GEORGE ELIOT, *ADAM BEDE*

But mercy is above this sceptered sway,
It is enthronèd in the hearts of kings,
It is an attribute to God himself...
                    —SHAKESPEARE, *THE MERCHANT OF VENICE*, ACT IV

Mercy within mercy within mercy.
                                        —THOMAS MERTON[29]

From poverty of spirit to mourning to meekness to hungering and thirsting for righteousness. And now to the beatitude of mercy.

One of the dangers of attempting to live a righteous life is that self-righteousness is always just a breath away. How easy it is to list the sins I haven't committed, to catalogue the sins of others, to fill pages with my own good deeds. This is the situation of the righteous man whom Christ describes in the parable about the Pharisee and the tax collector. The Pharisee thanked God that he was not like so many other people—thieves, cheats, adulterers—or like the tax collector in the back of the Temple. He reminded God that he fasted twice a week and gave away a tenth of his income, no small achievement then or now. Meanwhile the tax collector, overcome with awareness of his sins and his unworthiness to be in God's house or even to whisper God's name, beat his chest, begging for divine mercy (Lk 18:10-14). The tax collector's action is a seed of the Jesus

Prayer: "Lord Jesus Christ, Son of God, have mercy on me, a sinner."

Christ is constantly ready to be merciful to anyone because he is Mercy itself.

One of the turning points in human history was Abraham's discovery of God's mercy when he was poised to kill Isaac, his only child. Child sacrifice was common in Abraham's world. In a cosmos controlled by easily irritated and capricious deities, the more precious the sacrificial gift, the more the god to whom it was offered might be placated—like the dragon in the medieval legend of Saint George, who was presented with maidens in order to ward off attacks on the city. Given ordinary assumptions in his world, it may be that Abraham was not astonished at the prospect of such a heartbreaking sacrifice. But at the moment when Abraham's knife was poised to shed Isaac's blood, he heard an angel say, "Abraham, Abraham." He replied, "Here I am." The angel said, "Do not lay a hand on the boy or do him any harm, for now I know that you fear God, since you have not withheld your son, your only son, from me" (Gn 22:12). Abraham, the father of the Jewish people, had approached the border of child sacrifice and been turned away from it by God's command. Jews were to be unique in the Middle East not only because they were the people of the one God, but because they did not kill their children in order to ward off God's wrath. A man raised in a culture of ruthless, blood-drenched gods had encountered the merciful God.

In our world the word *mercy* is often used in a juridical context—a reporter might note that "the defendant threw himself on the mercy of the court." A clement judge, taking into account the particular circumstances of a crime, may decide not to punish a guilty person with the full severity of the law—a five-year sentence might be reduced by half or a person put on probation instead of behind bars.

The most commonly used Hebrew word for mercy, *khesed,* goes deeper. It can also be translated "tenderness," "kindness," "graciousness," "loving kindness," and "self-giving, unconditional love."

In the Greek New Testament the word used in the beatitude of mercy is *eleos*. We hear it in one of most repeated prayers in the Orthodox liturgy: "*Kyrie eleison*–Lord have mercy." It is linked to the Greek word *eleemosyne*: gracious deeds done for those in need, merciful giving, almsgiving. It also stands for all those inarticulate sounds associated with suffering–sighs, groans, moans, sobs, and laments.

In the Old Testament the word *mercy* is used either to describe an attribute of God–"All the paths of the LORD are mercy and truth" (Ps 25:10)–or as an appeal for God's help–"Have mercy on me, O God, in accordance with your great mercy" (Ps 51:1). Mercy is one of the divine energies revealed to all who love God, whose mercy "is infinite, reaching to the heavens" (Ps 36:5).

The Creator's mercy can rescue even those who have died: "You have delivered my soul from the depths of the grave" (Ps 86:13). This is the world Christ himself enters after his death on the cross. In the Orthodox church the most commonly displayed Paschal icon shows Christ standing on the smashed gates of hell, pulling Adam and Eve from their tombs. A text sung hundreds of times during the Paschal season rejoices that the mercy of God conquers even the grave: "Christ is risen from the dead, trampling down death by death, and upon those in the tombs bestowing life."

Mercy is central to Mary's hymn of praise for having been chosen to give birth to the Messiah:

> His mercy is on them who fear him
> from generation to generation. . . .
> He helps his servant Israel
>   to remind us of his mercy,
> just as he told our fathers,
>   Abraham and his seed, forever. (Lk 1:50, 54)

Twice in the gospels–in Matthew 9:13 and 12:7–Christ recalls the words of the prophet Hosea: "I desire mercy, not sacrifice" (Hos 6:6). He warns the scribes and Pharisees of the woe they bring upon themselves by concentrating on details of religious observance while "neglecting the weightier matters of the law: justice, mercy, and faith," thus "straining out a gnat and swallowing a camel" (Mt 23:23-24).

When those in desperate need seek his help, they cry out like the two blind men, "Have mercy on us, Son of David!" (Mt 9:27).

Christ teaches that those who seek God's mercy must pardon others. So essential is this principle that Christ includes it in the one prayer he teaches his disciples, "And forgive us our debts as we forgive our debtors." Each time we recite the Our Father, we ask the same measure of mercy from God that we give to others.

The same teaching is made even more vivid in the parable of the Good Samaritan. Asked the question, "Who is my neighbor?" Christ tells the story of a traveler whose life is saved not by two fellow Jews passing by on the other side of the road, but by a despised outsider, a Samaritan. Christ asks, "Which of the three, do you think, proved neighbor to the man who was beaten by robbers?" The man replies, "The one who showed mercy on him." Christ responds, "Go and do the same" (Lk 10:29-37).

Mercy may be essential to Christian life, yet it is far from a popular virtue. It seems more and more eroded, even in countries where Christianity is deeply rooted. In the United States, where criminal penalties in general are far more severe than in Europe, the death penalty has been reinstated in the majority of states and enjoys enormous, and passionate, public support, not least from Christians. If public hangings were resumed, it's a safe bet that they would be well attended and televised.

Still more chilling, killing by abortion and euthanasia is justified not on the straightforward grounds of convenience or economy but on claims of mercy and tenderness: we kill to end or prevent suffering. This led the novelist Flannery O'Connor to observe:

One of the tendencies of our age is to use suffering to discredit the goodness of God, and once you have discredited his goodness, you have done with him. The Alymers [after a fictional character created by Nathaniel Hawthorne; Alymer could not bear ugliness] . . . have multiplied. Busy cutting down human imperfection, they are making headway also on the raw material of good. Ivan Karamazov cannot believe [in God], as long as one child is in torment; Camus' hero cannot accept the divinity of Christ, because of the massacre of the innocents. In this popular pity, we mark our gain in sensibility and our loss in vision. If other ages felt less, they saw more, even if they saw with the blind, prophetical, unsentimental eye of acceptance, which is to say, of faith. In the absence of this faith now, we govern by tenderness. It is a tenderness which, long since cut off from the person of Christ, is wrapped in theory. When tenderness is detached from the source of tenderness, its logical outcome is terror. It ends in forced labor camps and in the fumes of the gas chamber.[30]

Few have taken so hard and so close a look at evil as the Russian author and prison-camp survivor Alexander Solzhenitsyn. Yet Solzhenitsyn insists that the human race is not divided between the good and the evil; rather that the division is in each of us. He writes:

The line separating good and evil passes not through states, nor between classes, nor between political parties either—but right through every human heart—and through all human hearts. This line shifts. Inside us, it oscillates with the years. And even within hearts overwhelmed by evil, one small bridgehead of good is retained. And even in the best of hearts, there remains . . . an un-uprooted small corner of evil.[31]

Not long ago I met a woman who had suddenly been made aware of that "un-uprooted corner of evil" in her own heart:

Donna Eddy, a teacher in Milwaukee. We were breakfast guests of a couple we both know. Over coffee she offered to explain why she was opposed to handguns and what had made her so active with the Coalition to Abolish the Death Penalty.

While still a college student, she had a pizza-delivery job. One night her job brought her face to face with three boys who demanded the money she was carrying. Two of them had small handguns—Saturday Night Specials, she later found out.

"All I had was twenty dollars belonging to the pizza company. It wasn't my money; I didn't care, but I didn't take them seriously. Those guns looked like toys to me. As far as I was concerned, they were just kids playing a game. So I just got back in the car. Then one of the boys pointed the gun at me and started to cry. 'But I could shoot you,' he pleaded. I decided I'd better give him the money, but he didn't give me a chance. He pulled the trigger. The gun made such a little noise, just a pop, not like what you hear in the movies. I felt this hot pain, like a pellet gun.

"Thank God those boys ran as fast as they did or I would have done some terrible harm to them. I gunned the engine and used my car as a weapon, chasing after them. It took me about ninety seconds to come to my senses. I thought to myself, What are you doing? If you catch up with them, are you going to run over them?

"So I drove to the police station, but all they did was tell me I was a fool for delivering pizzas in that part of town. I still didn't realize I had been bleeding—I told the police it was just a pellet gun. But they said a medic should take a look. It was only at the hospital that I realized that I'd been shot!"

Donna was lucky. The bullet had hit her belt buckle, angled off to the side, tunneled between two layers of skin, and then come back out. It was a superficial wound but a life-changing experience. "That was the day I learned I had the potential for that kind of violence. For ninety seconds of my life, primitive rage ruled. If I'd had a gun, at least one of those boys might be dead today."

Donna Eddy's story reminded me of a turning point in the early life of a recently canonized Orthodox saint, Silouan of Mount Athos. Born in Russia in 1866, Silouan was an uneducated peasant possessing considerable physical strength and, in his youth, a hot temper. During a feast day celebrating the patron saint of his village, he was playing a concertina when two brothers, the village cobblers, began to tease him. The older of the brothers tried to snatch the concertina from Silouan and a fight broke out.

"At first I thought of giving in to the fellow," Silouan related in later life, "but then I was ashamed at how the girls would laugh at me, so I gave him a great hard blow in the chest. His body shot away and he fell backwards with a heavy thud in the middle of the road. Froth and blood trickled from his mouth. All the onlookers were horrified. So was I. 'I've killed him,' I thought, and stood rooted to the spot. For a long time the cobbler lay where he was. It was over half an hour before he could rise to his feet. With difficulty they got him home, where he was bad for a couple of months, but he didn't die."

After that, Silouan felt that there was only the slightest difference between himself and a murderer. It was only thanks to God's mercy that he hadn't killed a neighbor. Perhaps it isn't surprising that afterward he found himself drawn to a life of prayer and penance.

After becoming a monk of Mount Athos in Greece, he thought and prayed deeply about violence and its causes. One of God's gifts to him was a profound sense of the oneness of the human race. He realized that, "through Christ's love, everyone is made an inseparable part of our own, eternal existence . . . for the Son of Man has taken within himself all mankind."

Much of Silouan's spiritual struggle centered on love of enemies, a goal that was unachievable without ardent prayer: "If we are incapable [of loving our enemies] and if we are without love, let us turn with ardent prayers to the Lord, to his Most Pure Mother, and to all the Saints, and the Lord will help us with everything, He whose love for us knows no bounds."[32]

Mercy is a hard virtue, even if it sounds like a soft quality. We want mercy for ourselves but resist extending it to others. We are eager to judge things we know little about or see from only one side. We tend to see ourselves in a good light. After all, we are more or less decent people with relatively good intentions. At least we aren't mass murderers or drug barons. But what Christ calls us to become is people living the mercy of God.

. . . for they shall obtain mercy.

In this beatitude the Savior speaks not only of those who show mercy by giving alms but of any form of mercy in action, for the ways of showing mercy are countless and this commandment is broad. What then is the promised reward? "For they shall obtain mercy." It seems to be a reward that equals our merciful deeds, but truly it is a far greater thing than any human act of goodness. For while they themselves show mercy as men, they obtain mercy from the God of all, and God's mercy is not the same thing as man's but is as wide as the gulf between wickedness and goodness, so far is the one of these removed from the other.

—SAINT JOHN CHRYSOSTOM[33]

For judgment is without mercy to one who has shown no mercy; yet mercy triumphs over judgment.

—SAINT JAMES (JAS 2:13)

What no eye has seen, nor ear heard,
nor the heart of man conceived,
what God has prepared for those who love him.

—SAINT PAUL PARAPHRASING ISAIAH (1 COR 2:9)

At the Last Judgment the merciful receive mercy: "Come, you blessed of my Father, inherit the kingdom prepared for you since the foundation of the world. . . . Truly I say to you, whatever you did to the least person, you did to me" (Mt 25:34, 40).

While Christ cites six merciful types of activity—feeding the hungry, giving drink to the thirsty, clothing the naked, providing hospitality to the homeless, caring for the sick, and visiting the prisoner—the works of mercy include any action of caring for others, especially those who are most easily ignored, dehumanized, or made into targets of wrath rather than love. (Dorothy Day often spoke of the spiritual works of mercy: admonishing the sinner, instructing the ignorant, counseling the doubtful, comforting the sorrowful, bearing wrongs patiently, forgiving all injuries, and praying for the living and the dead.)

In a section of *The Brothers Karamazov* that echoes the Last Judgment, Dostoevsky relates the story of a woman who was almost saved by a single onion:

> Once upon a time there was a woman, and she was wicked as wicked could be, and she died. And not one good deed was left behind her. The devils took her and threw her into the lake of fire. And her guardian angel stood thinking: what good deed of hers can I remember to tell God? Then he remembered and said to God: once she pulled up an onion and gave it to a beggar woman. And God answered: now take that same onion, hold it out to her in the lake, let her take hold of it, and pull, and if you pull her out of the lake, she can go to paradise, but if the onion breaks, she can stay where she is. The angel ran to the woman and held out the onion to her: here, woman, he said, take hold of it and I'll pull. And he began pulling carefully, and had almost pulled her all the way out, when other sinners in the lake saw her being pulled out and all began holding on to her so as to be pulled out with her. But the woman was wicked as wicked could be, and she began to kick them with her feet: "It's me who's getting pulled out, not you; it's my onion, not yours." No sooner did she say it then the onion broke. And the woman fell back into the lake and is burning there to this day. And the angel wept and went away.[34]

"Hell is not to love anymore," said Georges Bernanos. It is for those who prefer not to be in communion with others. For them, to be in heaven would be worse than hell. Why would you want to be with people forever whom you have spent every day of your life on earth avoiding?

But what of heaven? When the church Fathers searched the Bible for texts that reveal what communion with God is like, they often made what seems to us a surprising choice—the Song of Solomon, a collection of love poems, many of them erotic, written to be sung at weddings: "Your love is better than wine, your anointing oils are fragrant, your name is oil poured out. . . . Arise, my love, my fair one, and come away, for lo, the winter is past. . . . My beloved is mine and I am his." Page after page celebrates the primary joy man and woman take in each other in marital love.

The church Fathers, though themselves celibate, found in this ecstatic marital poetry the best metaphor we have for God's love: human love in its most pure, unreserved, and intense form. The difference is that the love of God is infinite and absolute, while ours is temporary and limited. God's mercy is like the burning bush, which blazes but is not consumed.

Blessed are the pure in heart...

Let mercy outweigh all else in you. Let compassion be a mirror where we may see in ourselves that likeness and that true image which belong to the Divine nature and Divine essence. A hard and unmerciful heart will never be pure.

—SAINT ISAAC OF SYRIA[35]

How else but through a broken heart
May Lord Christ enter in?

—OSCAR WILDE[36]

It is only with the heart that one can see rightly; what is essential is invisible to the eye.

—ANTOINE DE SAINT-EXUPÉRY[37]

Poverty of spirit, mourning, meekness, hungering and thirsting for righteousness, mercy—now, purity of heart. The beatitudes fold into each other. Mercy is inseparable from purity of heart.

What is a pure heart? A heart free of possessiveness, a heart capable of mourning, a heart that thirsts for what is right, a merciful heart, a loving heart, an undivided heart.

"The divided heart," Father James Silver commented in a recent letter, "is a symptom of distraction, even dissipation, of the soul, which desires one thing but behaves as if it desired another—the spiritual equivalent of wanting to have our cake and eat it too. Modern psychology describes this as 'self-defeating behavior' and 'lack of focus.'"

Spiritual virtues that defend the heart are memory, awareness, watchfulness, wakefulness, attention, hope, faith, and love.

Opposing purity of heart is lust of any kind—for wealth, for recognition, for power, for vengeance, for sexual access to others—whether indulged through action or imagination.

In classical Greek the word for "pure"—*katharos*—can be applied to anything without taint, stain, blemish, or impurity: a wine that has not been watered down, gold without alloy, fresh spring water clear as air, bread made of the best ingredients. It can also refer to language unpolluted by lies, half-truths, or slogans; it can signify a person without vices—an official who would never take a bribe, or a man who is perfectly truthful and straightforward. A related Greek word, *katharsis*, means "the act or process of purification," while *katharterion* is "a liquid with a purging effect," which can cleanse the body of disease.

In the Old Testament purity had to do primarily with ritual life and its disciplines: foods that could be eaten, or correctly performed ceremonial washings. Ritual purity required the observant Jew not to eat pork or shellfish, and to isolate dairy products from meat. Each month a woman in her childbearing years had to bathe in running water after her menstrual period ended; similarly, Gentile converts to Judaism, whether male or female, had to be baptized in the *mikvah* as part of their ritual initiation. On the Day of Atonement the high priest had to wash his entire body five times, his hands and feet ten times. Any male descendent of Aaron could be a priest, but only if his body had none of the 147 blemishes identified in the Law and he was not the son of a forbidden marriage.

But purity was seen not only as a physical condition but also as an inner quality: wholeness or integrity of spirit, an upright and blameless person, a clean heart, a person free of sin.

> Who shall ascend the hill of the LORD?
>   And who shall stand in his holy place?
> Those who have clean hands and pure hearts,
>   who do not lift up their souls to what is false,
>   and do not swear deceitfully. (Ps 24:3-4)

Blessed are the pure in heart...

Create in me a pure heart, O God,
  and put a new and right spirit within me.
                                    (Ps 51:10)

Without purity of heart, God tells Isaiah, prayers are not heard:

Even though you make many prayers,
  I will not listen,
  for your hands are blood-stained.

What are the requirements for purity? Isaiah's text continues:

Wash yourselves, make yourselves clean.
  Take away the evil from your souls before my
        eyes!
Cease to do evil,
  learn to do good!
Seek justice,
  correct oppression,
  defend the fatherless,
  plead for the widow. (Is 1:15-17)

In the gospels ritual purity is no longer a pressing issue, though the symbolism of a ritual bath was central to John the Baptist's call to repentance and was to become the foundational Christian sacrament.

Christ stresses purity of heart. He compares those who follow the laws of purity but lack mercy with whitewashed tombs: beautiful and clean on the outside but full of dead bones and the stench of death. A clean body is less important than a clean heart.

Remove every page with the word *heart* from an anthology of poetry, and you are left with a thin book. Homer proclaimed in *The Iliad:*

For I detest the doorways of Death, I detest that
      man, who

hides one thing in the depths of his heart, and
speaks forth another.[38]

Shakespeare declared in *King Henry the Sixth*:

What stronger breastplate than a heart untainted![39]

John Donne saw the heart as the place of divine encounter:

Batter my heart, three-personed God; for you
As yet but knock, breathe, shine, and seek to
mend.[40]

William Blake in *Songs of Innocence* wrote:

For Mercy has a human heart,
Pity, a human face,
And Love, the human form divine,
And Peace, the human dress.[41]

If you were to circle the word *heart* each time it appears in
the New Testament, your pencil would be kept busy page after
page. Among circled verses would be: "Where your treasure
is, there also is your heart" (Mt 6:21), "Unless you forgive your
brother from your heart" (Mt 18:35), "You must love the Lord
God with your whole heart" (Mt 22:37), "All those who heard
these words treasured them in their hearts" (Lk 1:66), "Mary
treasured all these things and pondered them in her heart" (Lk
2:19), "A good man draws what is good from the store of goodness in his heart" (Lk 6:45), "Did not our hearts burn within us
as he talked to us?" (Lk 24:32), and "Do not let your hearts be
troubled or afraid" (Jn 14:27).

Why such stress on the heart in the gospel? In our brain-
centered society it ought to surprise us that Christ didn't say,
"Blessed are the pure in mind," or better yet, "Blessed are the
brilliant in mind." We are, after all, a people who tend to re-

gard the brain as the core of the self—not the soul or heart. It's high praise to be described as "bright." Those recognized as clever have a shot at joining the aristocracy of the intelligent and may find themselves hugely rewarded. No one aspires to be labeled "slow" or "dense." It is a sign of the poverty of our culture that "stupid" is nearly a curse word or even a license to kill—a pregnant woman who knows she is bearing a child with Down's syndrome is often urged to have an abortion.

The brain has come up in the world while the heart has been demoted to a blood-providing muscle, a unidirectional pump. But, as metaphor, for thousands of years the heart has represented the hub of human identity and been linked with our capacity to love, the core not only of our physical but of our spiritual life.

The metaphorical meaning still holds fast even in our time. After identifying the heart as a muscle, *The American Heritage Dictionary* defines *heart* as "the vital center of one's being, emotions and sensibilities; the repository of one's deepest and sincerest feelings and beliefs."[42] According to the Russian author Boris Vysheslavtsev, "The heart is the center not only of consciousness but of the unconscious, not only of the soul but of the spirit, not only of the spirit but of the body, not only of the comprehensible but of the incomprehensible; in one word, it is the absolute center [of a human being]."[43]

We sense a pure heart in the face of any saintly person, and we catch glimpses of pure hearts in stories of saints who may have died many generations ago.

Consider one of the best loved saints of Russia, Seraphim of Sarov, a contemporary of Tsar Peter the Great, a man as meek as the tsar was mighty. I have never been in a Russian church that did not have Seraphim's icon.

Seraphim grew up in a merchant family in Kursk and had his first vision of the mother of God when he was nine and in danger of death after a fall from scaffolding. He began monastic life in 1778, when he was nineteen. Years later, after ordination as a priest in 1793, he received permission to live in solitude in a log cabin several miles from his community. It was, he said, his "Holy Land." Here he maintained a life of prayer, read the Bible, studied texts by and about the saints, tended his garden, chopped wood, and embraced austerities reminiscent of the Desert Fathers. Though he was once nearly beaten to death by three robbers who had heard there was a treasure hidden in his hermitage, he was never attacked by the wild animals he lived among. (When the assailants were later arrested, Seraphim tried to have them excused from their crime.) Visitors sometimes found him sharing his ration of bread with bears, wolves, lizards, and snakes. "How is it," he was asked, "that you have enough bread in your bag for all of them?" "There is always enough," Seraphim answered.

Late in his life his cabin became a place of pilgrimage—even Tsar Alexander I was among his guests.

One of those brought to him was a gravely ill landowner. "What, you have come to look upon poor Seraphim?" the hermit asked. After the man explained his condition, Seraphim prayed over him and the man was healed. In his joy he asked Seraphim how he could express his gratitude. Insisting that he had done nothing but pray and that only God can heal, Saint Seraphim advised the rich man to give away everything he possessed, free his serfs, and live in holy poverty. With all this the man complied. Some might regard the man's embracing of poverty as a greater miracle than the healing of his body.

In talks with visitors Saint Seraphim stressed "the acquisition of the Holy Spirit" so that the kingdom of God can take possession of the heart. A man of constant prayer and fasting, Seraphim reminded others that ascetic practice was only a means to a greater end: "Prayer, fasting, watching may be good in themselves; yet it is not in these practices alone that the goal of our Christian life is found, though they are necessary means for its attainment. The true goal consists in our acquiring the Holy Spirit of God." On occasion he put the message even more simply: "Acquire the Spirit of Peace, and thousands around you will be saved."

It is God alone, he taught, who warms the soul:

> God is fire that warms and kindles the heart and inward
> parts. And so, if we feel in our hearts coldness, which is
> from the devil–for the devil is cold–then let us call upon
> the Lord and he will come and warm our hearts with per-
> fect love not only for him but for our neighbor as well.
> And from the presence of warmth, the coldness of the
> hater of good will be driven way.[44]

Seraphim recognized kindness, joy, and the refusal to condemn others as signs of God's presence in the heart:

> You cannot be too gentle, too kind. Shun even to appear
> harsh in your treatment of each other. Joy, radiant joy,
> streams from the face of him who gives and kindles joy in
> the heart of him who receives. All condemnation is from
> the devil. Never condemn each other. We condemn oth-
> ers only because we shun knowing ourselves. When we
> gaze at our own failings, we see such a swamp that noth-
> ing in another can equal it. That is why we turn away,
> and make much of the faults of others. Instead of con-
> demning others, strive to reach inner peace. Keep silent,
> refrain from judgment. This will raise you above the deadly
> arrows of slander, insult, and outrage and will shield your
> glowing hearts against all evil.

At the core of Seraphim's spiritual life was Christ's resurrection. In his later years he wore white, the Paschal color, rather
than the usual monastic black. No matter what season of the
year, he was likely to greet visitors with the Paschal exclamation: "Christ is risen!" Paschal gladness affected even his way
of speaking to others–he addressed each of his spiritual children as "my joy."

When he died in 1833, at age seventy-one, Seraphim was at
prayer on his knees before an icon of the mother of God. He

had labored long and hard to free himself of all obstacles to God and finally was given a heart so pure that it seems no one can come near him, or kiss his icon, without being drawn toward purity of heart.[45]

Purification of the heart is the endless struggle of seeking a more God-centered life. It is the minute-to-minute discipline of trying to be so aware of God's presence that the heart has no space for our own worries, ambitions, or attention to appearances. Prayer is essential to this endeavor, whether reciting prayers we know by heart or spontaneous prayer or reading or music or using any of the senses with a heightened awareness of the sacred. Prayer refers to all we do in order to turn our attention toward God.

As with many saints, an indispensable element in Seraphim's life was the Jesus Prayer, also known as the Prayer of the Heart. Seraphim taught novices in his care, "Coming or going, sitting or standing, working or in church, let this prayer always be on your lips: 'Lord Jesus Christ, Son of God, have mercy on me, a sinner.' The whole art [of prayer] is there. With this prayer in your heart you will find inward peace and sobriety of body and soul."

The Prayer of the Heart has variations. Sometimes the words "a sinner" are dropped. At times it has even shorter forms: "Lord Jesus, have mercy on me," or even just these two words: "Jesus, mercy." Whatever the form, the prayer helps draw those who use it more and more deeply into the mercy of Christ. I sometimes say it in behalf of others: "Lord Jesus Christ, Son of God, have mercy on us *(or a person or group that is named)*." Monastic literature and practice refer to the prayer's full form as being "the whole gospel in one sentence."

There are those who recite the prayer so steadily that it becomes as integrated into life as breathing and the beating of the heart. Learning its use seems to have been a fundamental element in monastic life since the age of the Desert Fathers in the fourth century. A classic of the nineteenth century, *The Way of the Pilgrim*, describes how one wandering Russian, with the encouragement and guidance of a monk, learned to pray without ceasing using the Jesus Prayer. I once encountered a man in Moscow working in a small monastery shop who was whispering the Jesus Prayer as he counted out the change he was giving me.

Even for those of us who are far from constant prayer, the Jesus Prayer can become a part of daily life, secretly recited while walking, waiting in line, struggling with anger or depression, or lying in bed unable to sleep. Although at first it may seem an affectation and a distraction, it can soon become a guardian of inner silence and a way of being more—not less—attentive.

"Always keep your mind collected in your heart," instructed the great teacher of prayer Saint Theofan the Recluse. The Jesus Prayer is part of a tradition of spiritual life that helps move the center of consciousness from the mind to the heart. Neither the mind nor the heart should be considered only in physical terms. The mind represents the analytic and organizational aspect of consciousness, the heart that part of self most vulnerable to God's presence and most capable of experiencing God's love.[46]

Use of the Jesus Prayer is one simple way of guarding the soul from preoccupation with the faults, real or imagined, of others. "A person is truly pure of heart when he considers all human beings as good and no created thing appears impure or defiled to him," wrote Saint Isaac of Syria, also known as Isaac of Nineveh.[47]

The stories of the Desert Fathers are full of accounts of monks whose hardest combat was to overcome the hardness of heart that led them to judge and condemn others.

There is the story of two Egyptian monks who happened to come upon a woman stranded on one side of a stream too deep for her to cross. One of the monks picked her up and carried her safely to the other side—an action that scandalized the other monk. Finally, after walking a long distance in silence, he angrily chastised his brother for breaking the vow of chastity by touching a woman. The other monk replied, "I carried her across the river and put her down on the other side, but you are still carrying her."

A pure heart is one through which the mercy of God flows toward others, as is related in another story from the Egyptian desert. This one dates from the fourth or early fifth century:

A young brother went to an elder and confessed he was constantly enduring sexual fantasies, The older monk, who himself had been spared such temptations, told his visitor that he was not fit for monastic life. Agreeing that he was unworthy, the young man set out to return to the world. In God's providence Abbot Apollo was coming toward him, saw his despair, and questioned him about its cause. "Think it no strange thing, my son, and do not despair, for I too, even at my age and in this way of life, am hard pressed by just such thoughts as these," Abbot Apollo confessed. "Therefore do not give up when tested in this way. The remedy is not in our anxious thoughts but in God's compassion." The young monk took heart and returned to monastic life.

But the story goes further. Abbot Apollo walked directly to the cell of the monk who had been so lacking in compassion and stood silently outside his dwelling, praying that the elder would be visited by the same temptations the young man had suffered. His prayer was answered so quickly that before long the elder ran from his cell, walking as if he were drunk, going down the same road the young man had taken, convinced he could no longer be a monk. But Abbot Apollo stopped him, saying, "Go back to your cell, recognize your weakness, and look to yourself, for either the devil had forgotten you until now or was contemptuous of you, not finding in you someone worthy of battle. Did I say battle? You could not even withstand attack for a single day. But all this has befallen you because when the young man came to you for help against our common adversary, instead of anointing him with words of comfort, you sent him away in desperation."[48]

The more pure the heart, the more aware it is of the Creator in creation, taught one of the great saints of the Byzantine era, Saint Isaac of Syria. He laid great stress on ascetic struggle—prayer, fasting, voluntary poverty, generosity to the poor—as the way to purify the heart. A warrior against passions of the world, this bishop of the seventh century was passionate in his love of creation, not only the human being made in God's image but everything God has graced with life. He asked:

> What is purity? It is a heart full of compassion for the whole of created nature . . . And what is a compassionate heart? . . . It is a heart which burns for all creation, for the birds, for the beasts, for the devils, for every creature. When he thinks about them, when he looks at them, his eyes fill with tears. So strong, so violent is his compassion . . . that his heart breaks when he sees the pain and suffering of the humblest creature. That is why he prays with tears at every moment . . . for all the enemies of truth and for all who cause him harm, that they may be protected and forgiven. He prays even for serpents in the boundless compassion that wells up in his heart after God's likeness.[49]

One of the people of modern times whose heart was radiantly pure was the Russian pianist Maria Yudina. I have come to know her indirectly through the memoirs of her friend and one-time classmate, composer Dimitri Shostakovich, and also through Tatiana Voogd, a member of our parish who knew Yudina personally and has slept under her piano—"the most sheltered place in her apartment," she tells me.

It was Maria Yudina's fate to live through the Russian revolution and its aftermath, seeing many of her dearest friends and colleagues disappear into the Gulag. A fearless Christian, she wore a cross visibly even while teaching or performing in public—an affirmation of belief at a time when the price of a display of religious faith could be one's work, one's freedom, even one's life. She lived an ascetic life, wearing no cosmetics, spending little on herself, and dressing simply. "I had the impression that Yudina wore the same black dress during her entire long life, it was so worn and soiled," said Shostakovich.[50]

For Maria Yudina, music was a way of proclaiming her faith in a period when presses were more carefully policed than pianos. "Yudina saw music in a mystical light. For instance, she saw Bach's *Goldberg Variations* as a series of illustrations to the Holy Bible," said Shostakovich. "She always played as though she were giving a sermon."[51]

She not only performed piano works but paused during concerts to read the poetry of such writers as Boris Pasternak, who were unable to publish at the time.

She was notorious among friends for her inability to keep anything of value for herself. "She came to see me once," Shostakovich recalled, "and said that she was living in a miserable little room where she could neither work nor rest. So I signed a petition, I went to see various bureaucrats, I asked a lot of people to help, I took up a lot of people's time. With great difficulty we got an apartment for Yudina. You would think that everything was fine and that life could go on. A short time later she came to me again and asked for help in obtaining an apartment for herself. 'What? But we got an apartment for you. What do you need another one for?' 'I gave the apartment away to a poor old woman.'"[52]

Shostakovich heard that friends had made a loan to Yudina of five rubles. "I broke a window in my room, it's drafty and so cold, I can't live like that," she had told them. "Naturally, they gave her the money—it was winter. A while later they visited her, and it was as cold in her room as it was outside and the broken window was stuffed with a rag. 'How can this be, Maria Veniaminovna? We gave you money to fix the window.' And she replied, 'I gave it for the needs of the church.'"[53]

Shostakovich, who regarded religion as superstition, didn't approve. "The church may have various needs," he protested, "but the clergy doesn't sit around in the cold, after all, with broken windows. Self-denial should have a rational limit." He accused her of behaving like a *yurodivye*, the Russian word for a holy fool, a form of sanctity in the eyes of the church.

Her public profession of faith was not without cost. Despite her genius as a musician, from time to time she was banned from concert halls and not once in her life was she allowed to travel outside Russia. Shostakovich remembered:

Her religious position was under constant artillery and even cavalry attack [at the music school in Leningrad]. Serebriakov, the director then, had a habit of making so-called "raids of the light brigade." . . . He realized that Yudina was a first-class pianist, but he wasn't willing to risk his own position. One of the charges of the light brigade was made specifically against her. The cavalry rushed into Yudina's class and demanded of Yudina: "Do you believe in God?" She replied in the affirmative. "Was she promoting religious propaganda among her students?" She replied that the Constitution didn't forbid it. A few days later a transcript of the conversation made by "an unknown person" appeared in a Leningrad paper, which also printed a caricature—Yudina in nun's robes surrounded by kneeling students. And the caption was something about preachers appearing at the Conservatoire. The cavalry trod heavily, even though it was the light brigade. Naturally, Yudina was dismissed after that.[54]

From time to time she all but signed her own death warrant. Perhaps the most remarkable story in Shostakovich's memoir concerns one such incident:

In his final years, Stalin seemed more and more like a madman, and I think his superstition grew. The "Leader and Teacher" sat locked up in one of his many *dachas,* amusing himself in bizarre ways. They say he cut out pictures and photos from old magazines and newspapers, glued them onto paper, and hung them on the walls. . . . [He] didn't let anyone in to see him for days at a time. He listened to the radio a lot. Once Stalin called the Radio Committee, where the administration was, and asked if they had a record of Mozart's Piano Concerto No. 23, which had been heard on the radio the day before. "Played by Yudina," he added. They told Stalin that of course they had it. Actually, there was no record, the concert had been live. But they were afraid to say no to Stalin, no one ever knew what the consequences might be. A human life meant nothing to him. All you could do was agree, submit, be a yes-man, a yes-man to a madman.

Stalin demanded that they send the record with Yudina's performance of the Mozart to his *dacha*. The committee panicked, but they had to do something. They called in Yudina and an orchestra and recorded that night. Everyone was shaking with fright, except for Yudina, naturally. But she was a special case, that one, the ocean was only knee-deep for her.

Yudina later told me that they had to send the conductor home, he was so scared he couldn't think. They called another conductor, who trembled and got everything mixed up, confusing the orchestra. Only a third conductor was in any shape to finish the recording.

I think this is a unique event in the history of recording—I mean, changing conductors three times in one night. Anyway, the record was ready by morning. They made one single copy in record time and sent it to Stalin. Now that was a record. A record in yes-ing.

Soon after, Yudina received an envelope with twenty thousand rubles. She was told it came on the express orders of Stalin. Then she wrote him a letter. I know about this letter from her, and I know that the story seems improbable. Yudina had many quirks, but I can say this—she never lied. I'm certain that her story is true. Yudina wrote something like this in her letter: "I thank you, Joseph Vissarionovich, for your aid. I will pray for you day and night and ask the Lord to forgive your great sins before the people and the country. The Lord is merciful and He'll forgive you. I gave the money to the church that I attend."

And Yudina sent this suicidal letter to Stalin. He read it and didn't say a word, they expected at least a twitch of the eyebrow. Naturally, the order to arrest Yudina was prepared and the slightest grimace would have been enough to wipe away the last traces of her. But Stalin was silent and set the letter aside in silence. The anticipated movement of the eyebrows didn't come.

Nothing happened to Yudina. They say that her recording of the Mozart was on the record player when the "Leader and Teacher" was found dead in his *dacha*. It was the last thing he had listened to.[55]

Shostakovich found Yudina's open display of belief foolish, yet one senses within his complaints both envy and awe. In a time of heart-stopping fear, here was someone as fearless as Saint George before the dragon, someone who preferred giving away her few rubles to repairing her own broken window, who "published" with her own voice the poems of banned writers, who dared to tell Stalin that he was not beyond God's mercy and forgiveness. She had a large and pure heart. No wonder her grave in Moscow has been a place of pilgrimage ever since her death.

. . . for they shall see God.

For now we see in a mirror darkly, but then we shall see face to face. Now I know in part. Then I shall understand fully, even as I have been fully understood.

–SAINT PAUL (1 COR 13:12)

Beloved, we are God's children now. It does not yet appear what we shall be, but we know that when he appears, we shall be like him, for we shall see him as he is. And every one who thus hopes in him purifies himself as he is pure.

–SAINT JOHN (1 JN 3:2-3)

Abba Olympius, a monk of the Egyptian desert in the fourth century, was visited one day by a pagan priest from Scetis. Having seen firsthand the austere life Christian monks were leading, the priest asked Abba Olympius, "Since you live like this, do you not receive any visions from your God?" Abba Olympius said to him, "No." The pagan priest was amazed that despite so many hours of prayer both day and night and such self-imposed hardship, the monks were left in the dark. He said, "Truly, if you see nothing, then it is because you have impure thoughts in your hearts." Abba Olympius brought the visitor's words to the elders of the community. Far from denouncing the pagan priest for daring to judge the life of Christians, the elders "were filled with admiration and said this was true, for impure thoughts separated men from God."[56]

The struggle to purify the heart is not an end in itself but is founded in the hope of nothing less than seeing God, an aspiration voiced in one of the morning prayers used in the Orthodox church:

We praise, bless, hymn and thank you for bringing us out of the shadows of night and showing us again the light of day. In your goodness we beg you, cleanse us from our sins and accept our prayer in your great tenderness of heart, for we run to you, the merciful and all-powerful God. Illumine our hearts with the true Sun of Righteousness; enlighten our minds and guard all our senses, that walking uprightly as in the day in the way of your commandments, we may attain eternal life. For with you is the fountain of life and we will be made worthy of enjoying your unapproachable light. For you are our God, and to you we ascribe glory: to the Father and to the Son and to the Holy Spirit, now and ever and unto ages of ages.

Our hope is not only of perceiving God but taking joy in the radiance of God–"to be made worthy of enjoying the unapproachable light." There is no comparable happiness. Even the joy that lovers take in each other provides only an analogy. Christ in his parables uses the metaphor of the marriage feast, enriching the image of love between man and woman with the dimension of the community that surrounds and supports each marriage. To see God is to enter into the great joy of God's love, the dialogue of love within the holy Trinity. The greatest joy King David can imagine is to see God's face:

> As for me, I shall behold your face in righteousness;
> when I awake, I shall be satisfied with beholding
> your form. (Ps 17:15).

Moses begged to see "the glory of God" and his request was granted. "I will make all my goodness pass before you, and will proclaim before you my name, 'The LORD' [Yahweh: the Being, He Who Is]. . . . But you cannot see my face; for no one shall see me and live. . . . See, there is a place by me where you shall stand on the rock; and while my glory passes by I will put you in a cleft of the rock, and I will cover you with my hand" (Ex 33:18-22). It is in this encounter with God on Mount Sinai that Moses received the commandments and the covenant was forged.

Centuries later there is the prophet Elijah's encounter with God. Like Moses, he has taken shelter in a "cleft of a rock" and on the same mountain, though his experience of the divine Presence is very different. God appears to Elijah not in a rock-shattering wind, or in an earthquake, or in fire and lightning but in "a still small voice" (1 Kgs 19:11-12). Later in his life, Elijah is carried away to heaven on a chariot of fire (2 Kgs 2:11); the icon of the prophet's ascension is often found in Orthodox churches.

Building on both events, in the New Testament there is the showing of God's glory in Christ's transfiguration, when he stands between Moses and Elijah, an event witnessed by Peter, John, and James: "And he was transfigured before them, and his face shown like the sun, and his garments became white as light." The terrified apostles heard the voice of the Father saying, "This is my beloved Son, my chosen. Listen to him!" (Mt 17:2-5). Elsewhere Christ declares, "Whoever has seen me has seen the Father" (Jn 14:9).

Orthodox theology speaks of the "light" the apostles saw as something other than sunlight; it is the splendor of the divine nature, "the uncreated light." Icons provide a silent, nonverbal tradition of communicating the kingdom of God, seeking to reveal through color and line what is inaccessible to photography. While iconographers have used various ways of suggesting "the uncreated light" that Christ radiated in the transfiguration, what best communicates the experience is not the rays and colors that surround Christ but the apostles' responses. Peter, John, and James are often shown as if thrown down by an earthquake, hiding their faces as they might from an explosion of light. In another version of the icon, one apostle is shown hiding his face while the two others are drawn closer to Christ, like leaves reaching toward the sun. Each apostle provides an image of transfigured life in which "it is no longer I who live, but Christ who lives in me" (Gal 2:20).

Among many remarkable stories left to us about Saint Seraphim of Sarov's life, perhaps the most amazing comes from the diary of Nicholas Motovilov. As a young man he came to Seraphim's hermitage seeking advice. At a certain point in their conversation, Seraphim said to his guest, "Look at me." Motovilov replied, "I am not able, Father, for there is lightning flashing in your eyes. Your face has grown more radiant than the sun and my eyes cannot bear the pain." Seraphim answered, "Do not be afraid, my dear lover of God, you have also now become as radiant as I. You yourself are now in the fullness of the Holy Spirit. Otherwise you would not be able to perceive me in the exact same state." Saint Seraphim then asked him how he felt. "I feel a great calm in my soul, a peace which no words can express. I feel an amazing happiness."[57]

C. S. Lewis manages to suggest the uncreated light in *The Great Divorce*, his imaginative account of a group of argumentative people on a day trip from hell to heaven. The fires of hell for Lewis are in the proud, unloving egos of its inhabitants, living in permanent gray twilight in what looks like a vast, run-down district of London. We discover in the first pages of this small book that few in hell are even interested in the journey—most regard heaven as overrated or nonexistent; but the monotony of hell, or the desire to prove hell's superiority, induces some of the local populace to board a tour bus and have a look. Much to their annoyance, however, it turns out that the bus doesn't go all the way to heaven. At a certain point it's necessary to get out and walk. Still worse, it is not an easy walk. The closer one gets to heaven, the more real and intense everything gets. Each line becomes sharper, each blade of grass more razor-edged, each ray of light more piercing, each breath of air more pure. We find that few of hell's visitors can go very far.

"Hell is a state of mind," Lewis writes. "But heaven is not a state of mind. Heaven is reality itself. All that is fully real is heavenly."[58]

Blessed are the peacemakers . . .

Our life and our death is with our neighbor. If we gain our brother, we have gained God, but if we scandalize our brother, we have sinned against Christ.

—SAINT ANTHONY THE GREAT[59]

An elder said, "I have spent twenty years fighting to see all human beings as one."

—SAYINGS OF THOSE WHO GREW OLD IN ASCESIS[60]

Only after ascending the first six rungs of the ladder of the beatitudes do we reach the beatitude of the peacemaker, for only a person who has taken all the steps that purify the heart can help rebuild broken bridges, pull down walls of division, assist us in recovering a small degree of our lost communion with God and with one another.

A few years ago in Moscow I had the opportunity to watch two restorers cleaning a large icon of Saint Nicholas. It was laid out on a table just outside the pastor's office. They estimated the dark panel was three hundred years old. As decades passed and thousands of candles burned before it, the image had become increasingly hidden under smoke-absorbing varnish until it was almost black. Using alcohol and balls of cotton, their gentle, painstaking efforts gradually revealed sharp lines and bright colors that brought the icon back to life. I felt I was witnessing a small resurrection.

Words, like icons, can reach a point where restoration is urgently needed. The word *peace* has been on the receiving end of a great deal of political smoke. In America, the Strategic Air

Command, one of the world's principal instruments for waging nuclear war, has as its motto, "Peace is our profession." In the former Soviet Union, the Russian word for peace—MIP (pronounced mir)—served as a one-syllable summary of all the policies and programs of the Kremlin, from the harassment and imprisonment of dissenters to whatever wars the leaders had decided served their interests. To this day, years after the collapse of the USSR, the word *peace* is hard to use in Russia. "It still has a Soviet smell to it," a friend in Moscow, Karina Cherniak, explained to me. "It is a word that reminds us of lies, fear, propaganda, and military parades—things that are the opposite of peace."

One way to restore the word is to see how *peace* is used in the Bible. In Hebrew, it is *shalom*, meaning a condition of perfect welfare, serenity, prosperity, happiness, and peaceful relations among people. "For the peace of Jerusalem pray," King David sings in Psalm 122. He is asking not only that Jerusalem be spared from war or strife within its walls but that every good gift might descend on the city.

Eirene, the word used in the Greek New Testament, describes God's ultimate blessing.

Throughout the gospel we see Christ conferring peace on his disciples. He tells the bearers of the gospel that, upon entering a dwelling, their first action should be a blessing, "Peace be upon this house" (Lk 10:5). In his final discourse before his arrest, he says to the apostles: "Peace I leave with you, my peace I give to you. Let not your hearts be troubled, neither let them be afraid" (Jn 14:27). After the resurrection he greets his followers with the words, "Peace be with you" (Lk 24:36; Jn 20:19).

The letters of the New Testament often begin with a blessing of peace—"Grace and peace to you from God our Father and the Lord Jesus Christ," writes Saint Paul to the young church in Corinth (1 Cor 1:3). Addressing the Christians in Rome, he reminds them "how beautiful are the feet of those who preach the Gospel of peace" (Rom 10:15). In the same letter he points out that "the kingdom of God is not meat and drink but righteousness and peace and joy in the Holy Spirit. . . . Let us therefore follow after those things which make for peace" (Rom 14:17, 19). Writing to the Ephesians, he explains that peace is not an abstraction but Christ himself: "For he is our peace, who has made us both one, and has broken down the dividing wall of enmity" (Eph 2:14). He teaches the Colossians that Christ "has reconciled all things to himself, having made peace through the blood of the Cross" (Col 1:20). In Paul's second letter to Timothy, there is his counsel to "shun youthful passions and aim at righteousness, faith, love and peace, along with those who call upon the Lord from a pure heart" (2 Tm 2:22).

Another way to restore the word *peace* is to consider its uses in the Orthodox liturgy, which still includes various litanies that were discarded in other churches in order to shorten the services. In the liturgy of Saint John Chrysostom, the most commonly used text, peace is one of the primary themes. The service begins with the priest's announcement, "Blessed is the kingdom of the Father, Son, and Holy Spirit." It is the perfect beginning, for the liturgy is a doorway into the kingdom of God, where peace rules.

The words that immediately follow are: "In peace let us pray to the Lord." Peace is the precondition of worship. This declaration, explained Father Lev Gillet,

> means first of all that we are called to assume a state of inner peace. Those who will take part in the Divine Liturgy should rid their minds of all confusion, all susceptibility to fleshly and earthly temptations, all obsession with "worldly cares," all hostile feelings towards any other person, and all personal anxiety. They should come before God in a state of inner calmness, trusting attentiveness, and single-minded concentration on "the one thing needful" (Lk 10:42).[61]

The opening litany is a series of appeals for peace:

For the peace from above, and the salvation of our souls.
. . . For the peace of the whole world, for the welfare of
the holy churches of God, and for the union of all. . . . For
seasonable weather, for abundance of the fruits of the
earth, and for peaceful times. . . . For our deliverance from
all affliction, wrath, danger and necessity. . . . Help us,
save us, and have mercy on us, and keep us, O God, by
your grace.

Here, *peace* refers to every possible blessing: salvation, unity,
plentiful food, good weather, peace among nations, relief from
hard times.

Repeatedly during the service the priest offers a blessing of
peace to all who are present, and they immediately return the
blessing to him. The gospel reading is introduced with the
words, "Peace be unto all." Then, in the litany of supplication,
we appeal to God "that the whole day may be perfect, holy,
peaceful and sinless." We ask for "an angel of peace, a faithful
guide, a guardian of our souls and bodies." We call on God for
"all things that are good and profitable for our souls, and for
peace in the world." We ask God's blessing "that we may complete the remaining time of our life in peace and repentance."
Later we are summoned to "stand upright and stand in fear . . .
that we may offer the Holy Oblation in peace." The choir responds, "A mercy of peace! A sacrifice of praise!"

Finally, at the end of the liturgy, whether in the Orthodox or
Catholic tradition, the priest tells us to "depart in peace." The
word *Mass* comes from the Latin form of this declaration: "Ite
missa est." The reason is clear. Having been privileged to take
part in the eucharist, we are returned to the world as ambassadors of Christ's peace among those who, in many cases, hardly
know who Christ is.

From both the gospel and the liturgy we learn that peace is
not a principle, theory, concept, political program, or social
ideal but is Christ himself: Christ who heals, Christ who forgives, Christ who reaches out to the very people, according

to the advice of the world, we should avoid, condemn, and hate.

Among the things that Christ did *not* say in the sermon on the mount is, "Blessed are those who prefer peace, wish for peace, await peace, love peace, or praise peace." His blessing is on the *makers* of peace. He requires an active rather than a passive role. In fact, peace itself is a dynamic state that can be anything but peaceful from the point of view of those who wish people would simply be quiet and do what is expected of them by whoever happens to be in charge.

Christ's peace is not placid. He is at his most paradoxical when he says, "Do not think that I have come to bring peace to the earth; I have not come to bring peace, but a sword" (Mt 10:34).[62]

Unfortunately, for most of us peace is not the kingdom of God but a slightly improved version of the world we already have. We would like to get rid of conflict without eliminating the factors, spiritual and material, that create division.

Many regard the Prince of Peace as a disturber of the peace. We see how unsettling Christ's peace is when we notice how much turmoil surrounds the events related in the gospel. Freeing an afflicted man from a demon, he sends the evil spirit into a herd of pigs, who in turn race into the lake and drown themselves; the local people, owners of the pigs, appeal to Christ to leave them alone. Among pious Jews, many are offended because he heals people on the Sabbath—could he not do these things any other day of the week? In healing the blind and paralyzed, he was stripping them of their livelihood as beggars; their daily bread would never again come so easily. Christ's cleansing of the Temple in Jerusalem involves overturning tables and expelling the moneychangers. Even the raising of Lazarus is resisted by Mary and Martha and the friends mourning with them—"Don't open the tomb! By now his body is stinking."

No saint has been more identified with the beatitude of peacemaking than Saint Francis of Assisi. The most famous prayer for peace, echoing the seventh beatitude, is attributed to him:

"Lord, make me an instrument of your peace." Whether or not these exact words were said by Francis, the prayer sums up his life and at the same time illustrates how disturbing Christ's peace can be to those who are basically pleased with the way things are.

As a young man Francis seemed well on his way to realizing all of his father's expectations: he was attractive, ambitious, popular among his peers, useful in his father's cloth shop on Assisi's main square, so well dressed that he was a walking advertisement for his father's wares. However, his life began to change course after a year-long period of imprisonment following a battle with the neighboring town of Perugia in the year 1202. Francis, then twenty years old, was lucky not to have been among the many maimed or killed in the fighting. He had imagined the glory of battle and of being a man-of-arms for years, but now he had seen the reality of war: hatred turning beautiful faces into hideous masks, twisting sane minds to madness. Freed at last by payment of a ransom, he returned home disillusioned and gravely ill. He spent months recovering.

The first glimpse we have of the transformation taking place in Francis's soul happened when he was riding outside the town and came upon a young man whose family had lost its property and fortune because of the war. All they had left was a ruined tower. The youth wore rags. Francis got off his horse and gave away his own splendid clothing.

Then there was the day he stopped to pray in the chapel of San Damiano. The building was in the final stages of decay, but it still possessed a large, cross-shaped image of the crucifixion painted in the ancient iconographic tradition, thus an image stressing less the suffering of Christ than his free gift of himself. Having given up dreams of glory in war, and finding moneymaking and spending a circular path going nowhere, he was desperate to have some sign of what God wanted him to do. Then, in the darkness, he heard Christ whisper to him, as if the icon itself were speaking: "Francis, go and repair my house, which, as you see, is falling into ruin."[63]

Taking the words literally, Francis set about the hard labor of rebuilding a chapel that no one else regarded as needed, financing the project by selling off some valuable items from his father's warehouse. This unauthorized action caused an explosion of paternal wrath that culminated in a trial before the bishop in Assisi's marketplace. Francis not only admitted his fault and restored his father's money but removed all his garments, presenting them to his father with the words, "Hitherto I have called you father on earth; but now I say, 'Our Father, who art in Heaven.'" The astonished bishop hastily covered Francis with his own mantle. Thus Francis cut the last threads binding him to the ambitions that had dominated his earlier life.

By now Francis had only one ambition: to live according to the gospel. He understood this to mean a life without money, wearing the same rags beggars wore, and owning nothing that might stir up the envy of others and thus give rise to violence. He wanted to be one of the least, a little brother living in poverty, rather than a great man.

What was most surprising was the spirit of joy that surrounded Francis. His customary greeting to those he met was "pace e bene"–"peace and goodness." Before long a dozen friends joined him, forming the nucleus of a new order, the *Minores* (the Lesser Brothers, in contrast to the *Majores*, the great ones who ruled the cities and organized wars). They were not simply poor but had, he explained, married the most beautiful bride, Lady Poverty. Assisi's bishop didn't approve. "You and your brothers are a disgrace," he told Francis. "At least you can provide what will make you a bit more respectable." "O Domini mi," replied Francis, "if we had possessions we should need weapons to protect them."

In 1210 the brothers walked to Rome and won approval for their simple rule of life from Pope Innocent III–this despite advice the pope had received that such absolute poverty as Francis's rule decreed was impractical. Legend explains that Pope Innocent had a dream of Francis in his rags preventing Rome's principal church from collapsing.

Francis, then twenty-eight, was to live only another sixteen years, but in his short life he left us with a treasure chest of stories about what can happen when someone tries with every fiber of his being to live the peace of Christ in the face of the world's violence.

Among the most well-attested stories in Francis's life is his meeting in 1219 with one of Christianity's chief opponents, Sultan Malik-al-Kamil. It was the time of the Fifth Crusade, shortly after a crusader victory at the port city of Damietta (modern Dumyat) on the Nile Delta. Francis, who opposed all killing no matter what the cause, sought the blessing of the cardinal who was chaplain to the crusader forces to go and preach the gospel to the sultan. The cardinal told him that the Muslims understood only weapons and that the one useful thing a Christian could do was to kill them. At last the cardinal stood aside, certain that Francis and Illuminato, the brother traveling with him, were being led to die as martyrs. The two left the crusader encampment singing the psalm, "The Lord is my shepherd . . . "

Soldiers of the sultan's army captured the pair, beat them, and then brought them before Malik-al-Kamil, who asked if they wished to become Muslims. Saying yes would save their lives. Francis replied that they came to seek his conversion; if they failed in their effort, then let them be beheaded. According to legend, Francis offered to enter a furnace to demonstrate the truth of Christ's gospel; whether or not he made such a proposal, going unarmed into the enemy's stronghold was analogous to leaping into a fire.

For a month Francis and the sultan met daily. Though neither converted the other, the sultan had such warmth for his guests that not only did he spare their lives but gave them a passport allowing them to visit Christian holy places under Muslim control and presented Francis with a beautifully carved ivory horn, which is now among the relics of the saint kept in the Basilica of Assisi. It is recorded that "the two [Francis and Malik-al-Kamil] parted as brothers."[64]

What a different history we would look back upon if Muslims had encountered Christians who did not slaughter their enemies. When the crusaders took Jerusalem in 1099 during the First Crusade, no inhabitant of the city was spared—men, women, and children were hacked to pieces until, the chronicle says, the crusaders' horses waded in blood. While Christians in the first three centuries would have taken a nonviolent example for granted, by the thirteenth century Francis was a voice crying in the wilderness. Christianity in the West was preaching the holiness of war.

Another of Francis's efforts as a peacemaker comes toward the end of his life and concerns Gubbio, a town north of Assisi. The people of Gubbio were troubled by a huge wolf that attacked not only animals but people, so that the men had to arm themselves before going outside the town walls. They felt as if Gubbio were under siege.

Francis decided to help, though the local people, fearing for his life, tried to dissuade him. What chance could an unarmed man have against a wild animal with no conscience? But according to the *Fioretti*, the principal collection of stories of the saint's life,

> Francis placed his hope in the Lord Jesus Christ, master of all creatures. Protected neither by shield or helmet, only arming himself with the sign of the Cross, he bravely set out of the town with his companion, putting his faith in the Lord who makes those who believe in him walk without injury on an asp . . . and trample not merely on a wolf but even a lion and a dragon.

Some local peasants followed the two brothers, keeping a safe distance. Finally the wolf saw Francis and came running, as if to attack him. The story continues:

> The saint made the sign of the Cross, and the power of God . . . stopped the wolf, making it slow down and close

its cruel mouth. Then Francis called to it, "Brother Wolf, in the name of Jesus Christ, I order you not to hurt me or anyone."

The wolf then came close to Francis, lowered its head and then lay down at his feet as though it had become a lamb. Francis then censured the wolf for its former cruelties, especially for killing human beings made in the image of God, thus making a whole town into its deadly enemy.

"But, Brother Wolf, I want to make peace between you and them, so that they will not be harmed by you any more, and after they have forgiven you your past crimes, neither men nor dogs will pursue you anymore."

The wolf responded with gestures of submission "showing that it willingly accepted what the saint had said and would observe it."

Francis promised the wolf that the people of Gubbio would henceforth "give you food every day as long as you shall live, so that you will never again suffer hunger." In return, the wolf had to give up attacking both animal and man. "And as Saint Francis held out his hand to receive the pledge, the wolf also raised its front paw and meekly and gently put it in Saint Francis's hand as a sign that it had given its pledge."

Francis led the wolf back into Gubbio, where the people of the town met them in the market square. Here Francis preached a sermon in which he said calamities were permitted by God because of our sins and that the fires of hell are far worse than the jaws of a wolf, which can only kill the body. He called on the people to do penance in order to be "free from the wolf in this world and from the devouring fire of hell in the next world." He assured them that the wolf standing at his side would now live in peace with them, but that they were obliged to feed him every day. He pledged himself as "bondsman for Brother Wolf."

After living peacefully within the walls of Gubbio for two years, "the wolf grew old and died, and the people were sorry, because whenever it went through the town, its peaceful kindness and patience reminded them of the virtues and holiness of Saint Francis."[65]

Is it possible that the story is true? Or is the wolf a storyteller's metaphor for violent men? While the story works on both levels, there is reason to believe there was indeed a wolf of Gubbio. A Franciscan friend, Sister Rosemary Lynch, tells me that during restoration work the bones of a wolf were found buried within the church in Gubbio.

While the encounters with the sultan and the wolf were later embellished, nonetheless certain aspects of both stories shine through the embroidery. In each instance Francis gave an example of love that refuses weapons. His courage is impressive; he was not only praying for enemies but meeting them, even at the risk of his own life. After all, to die in war for the kings of this earth has been the fate of millions of people; why should those who serve the gospel hesitate to risk their lives for the king of heaven?

Francis became, in a sense, the soldier he had dreamed of becoming as a boy; he was just as willing as the bravest soldier to lay down his life in defense of others. There was only this crucial difference. His purpose was not the conquest but the conversion of his adversary; this required refusing the use of weapons of war, because no one has ever been converted by violence. Francis always regarded conversion as a realistic goal. After all, if God could convert Francis, anyone might be converted. But such actions—equivalent to leaping into a furnace—are only possible when nothing in life is more important than Christ and his kingdom, a discipleship that begins with poverty of spirit and ascends to being an ambassador of Christ's peace.

"They are truly peacemakers," Saint Francis wrote in his *Admonitions*, "who are able to preserve their peace of mind and heart for love of our Lord Jesus Christ, despite all that they suffer in this world."

When I think of people I have known personally who in various ways have shown a similar love and courage, a similar commitment to conversion, one of the people who springs to mind is Sister Rosemary Lynch, the Franciscan who assured me there really was a wolf of Gubbio. Now in her eighties, she has been a Franciscan since she was seventeen. She and another Franciscan, Sister Klaryta Antoszewska, live in Las Vegas. Their Las Vegas isn't the familiar gambler's mecca of bright lights and roulette wheels but of people who clean hotel rooms, work in laundries, clear tables, and wash dishes.

Those who meet Rosemary are impressed with her radiant smile and the interest she takes in others, no matter how minor their position in life. She tends to call people "Honey." Though she is preoccupied with some of the most troubling problems in the world, I have rarely met anyone over the age of ten so free of anxiety, a trait she credits to her parents. She recalls that, as a child, she misunderstood the words of a certain hymn. "The hymn started off, 'O Lord, I am not worthy,' but for years I thought the words were, 'O Lord, I am not *worried!*' And actually, in our home, that was our attitude toward the Lord and toward life. We weren't worried—not about the Lord or anything else."

Saint Francis inspired her from an early age. "He was almost a member of my family. In our home we had an understanding of that marvelous universality, that cosmic love, that integrity of creation that are at the heart of Saint Francis. While we didn't fully understand how radical Francis was and what a reformation he started, in our home Francis hadn't landed in the bird bath."

In 1985, when Rosemary and I were teaching a course entitled "Making Peace, Serving Peace" at the Ecumenical Institute near Jerusalem, I asked her if seventeen hadn't been too young an age to commit herself to a religious community.

"Not at all," she assured me. "In those days we started just about everything younger. We took responsibility in our teens. It's a pity that nowadays we seem to be developing a culture of permanent immaturity, permanent dependency. You find university students who haven't the remotest idea what they want to do with their life. But when I was young, people had a goal that they were going toward. And this is what you still find among the refugee children."

Rosemary says the most important educational experience in her life began in 1960 when she was elected to serve at her congregation's headquarters in Rome, her home for sixteen years. "That's where I lived, but actually I was traveling a lot, months at a time. I would be visiting the different places where our sisters were working—Europe, North America, Mexico, Africa, and Southeast Asia. I began to look at the world with different eyes. One of the life-changing events was my first encounter with starvation. I happened to be in Tanzania during a drought. For the first time I was *surrounded* by starving children. It was a conversion experience—the realization that things were terribly out of place in the world. For months afterward I could hardly enter a store in the consumer society of Rome and see all those nonessentials and all the people buying them. I wanted to scream out loud, 'Doesn't anyone know that I saw a child die of hunger—and you are buying false eyelashes!'"

Rosemary and Klaryta's work in Las Vegas centers on refugees, immigrant families, prisoners, and peace.

"We try to do these things on two levels, to combine immediate, necessary work in the community and work to change structures that cause suffering. Working with refugees, we have tried to change the notion of the State Welfare Board, which was denying refugees financial help. Visiting prisoners, we have worked for a pre-trial release program. Working for peace, we not only try to get rid of nuclear weapons but also to help victims of Nevada's many nuclear tests. We don't want just to apply band-aids, but neither do we want to lose contact with people by becoming too abstract."

In the years when nuclear weapons were still being tested in mine shafts beneath the desert, Rosemary spent hundreds of hours standing in prayer on a highway adjacent to the nuclear test site and many more hours meeting with test-site employ-ees. She helped initiate Desert Witness, which each Lent brought thousands of people to fast and pray at the nuclear test site until the explosions finally stopped. Time and again she crossed the property line and was arrested.

Despite her many arrests, Sister Rosemary won the respect of people who were among the most law-abiding citizens. In 1985 the governor of Nevada and the mayor of Las Vegas hon-ored her with an officially proclaimed Rosemary Lynch Day. (However, not all the responses to Rosemary's efforts were so appreciative. In February 1988, following another arrest at the nuclear test site, she lost her job with a social service agency. "I have observed that the more deeply a person enters into this endeavor of peace-serving," she wrote the agency's director, "the more the cost of discipleship goes up. For me to abandon my hours of prayer and fasting in the desert would be a be-trayal of my own conscience.")

Rosemary sees her peace activities as a continuation of the renewal of Christianity associated with Saint Francis. "Not only were the brothers and sisters forbidden to have weapons or to use them for any reason," she often explains, "but so were the lay people who followed the rule he wrote for those living a family life."

In 1989 she and several co-workers decided to focus more intensively on nonviolence as a means of personal and social transformation, founding a group that took its name from a phrase often used by Saint Francis: *Pace e Bene* (peace and good-ness). "Even if nuclear weapons were abolished," Rosemary points out, "unless we defuse the bombs in our own hearts, the human family is quite capable of finding other even worse means of destroying life."

The refugees Klaryta and Rosemary received in the days when the United States was geared for war with the Soviet Union were a young Russian couple and their son. They had been given permission to leave because they had Jewish family back-grounds, though they were not active in synagogue or church.

"The man was a sculptor and graphics artist," Rosemary recalled, "the woman a restorer of icons and an illustrator of children's books–skills not in demand in Las Vegas! In the man's case it seemed Sister Klaryta was lucky–she found him a job in a graphics studio, but all we could get for the woman was a job as a 'bus person,' clearing tables in a casino restaurant. It was a humiliating job for a sensitive woman and skilled artist. She accepted it, but it was very hard.

"We had found them a small apartment, but they often knocked on our door. We would make a pot of good strong tea and talk for hours. For both husband and wife it soon became obvious that they couldn't continue with their jobs. It turned out that this 'art studio' wanted the husband to make posters for pornographic movies. But for him art is a sacred thing. This violated the nature of his being. We told him he had to stop.

"In his wife's case, the crisis was caused by a state law requiring that bread left on the table must be thrown out, even if no one has touched it. She came home one night completely broken, in tears, saying, 'They make me throw away the body of Christ!'

"That night I finally understood something basic in Slavic culture. They understand that *all* bread is holy, *all* bread is linked to the body of Jesus, not only bread consecrated on the altar. I'm sure our ancestors knew this too, but in the degenerate society that we now have, we no longer see this. We can easily throw bread into the garbage. But our friend could no longer violate her heart and her spirit by throwing away bread. So we told her, 'You have to stop immediately.' And she did. Finally Klaryta arranged for the family to go to New York, where there is a large Russian community and a much better chance to work as artists and icon restorers. It has never been very happy for them, but at least it's better than it was."

Rosemary regards her activities not as making peace but being in "the service of peace." As she says, "None of us can make peace. Peace is God's gift. But we can serve God's peace."

Nuclear weapons and warfare were not at all in her thoughts when she moved to Las Vegas. "But in Nevada, where so many nuclear weapons have exploded, you can't *not* think about what a nuclear war would mean. Thank God so far there has been no World War III, but we have many victims of the preparations for World War III. They are all around us. Some are the people working at the testing site, where the cancer rate is much higher than the national average. Many employees have been radiated in nuclear accidents. In addition there are all those soldiers who were close to ground zero when there were aboveground tests. Many have died already, and many have had defective children—the greatest sorrow. There are also the 'downwind victims' who were in the path of fallout clouds."

Rosemary's focus has always been on people, not weapons. "Of course we hope our efforts make it more likely that the day will come when there will be no more testing and no nuclear weapons, but what we are doing has another, deeper meaning—the recognition that we too, not only those making and testing weapons, are in need of *conversion*. Our motto has always been, 'Convert!' What we are doing concerns conversion. We need to convert our own hearts. As long as the bombs are exploding in our hearts, we have little hope of even understanding what is going on in the world around us. We hope not only for our own conversion but for a conversion that will lead our whole society in a new direction. The desert is a place linked to conversion. The desert has always been the classical place of spiritual solitude. The prophets of old searched for the voice of God in the desert. This is true for us too. So we go out to the desert to fast and pray. In the winter it is often windy and frigid, but in the warmer seasons it comes to life. You should see the desert at Easter time!"

Rosemary has developed a profound sympathy for those who work at the test site, many of whom she has come to know personally. "They are hostages of the bomb, just as we are," she comments. "Many friendships have taken root, especially with guards and police. Many people working at the site wave to us. I remember one worker who brought us a box of fresh donuts. He said, 'I may be on the other side, but I have to admire your perseverance.' Sometimes I am asked to help with very complex personal and family problems. There are people involved with nuclear weapons who have called me late at night with some personal crisis they needed to discuss. I have had sheriffs and military officers cry on my shoulder."

"Isn't there the danger of abusing people's vulnerability in such situations?" I asked. She told me, "I never say to them, 'You should quit.' I don't have the right. This is something you have to come to on your own. With the economic situation in the country so bad, many are glad to have a job, no matter what it is. Even so, some have left the test site, even at the cost of a lot of personal and family sacrifice."

When I asked how she justified breaking the law, she responded: "The real evil is perfecting methods of killing people and destroying God's creation. Breaking a trespass law—crossing a white line in a road miles from the test site—respects the essence of civil law and is obedience to the higher law. Sometimes the law needs help. Of course, you have to have a certain amount of openness and patience with people who don't see this and you must be willing to go to jail, which gives you a chance to 'visit the prisoner,' as Christ told us to do. But civil disobedience isn't for everyone. It is a call, a vocation. I would never say to anyone, 'You should do this.' But I ask others to respect the force of conscience that compels us who commit civil disobedience.

"We always practice openness with the police and everyone concerned about what we are doing. One consequence of this is that the police have always been gentle and courteous with us. They have even had a sense of the joy of the occasion. They try not to hurt us when they put on the handcuffs. They assist us getting into the police buses. It's remarkable."

Rosemary urges those who commit acts of disobedience to respect those who may feel threatened or be inconvenienced by such actions and to carefully avoid sarcasm, abrasive words, or rude gestures. "It is our policy never to have the kind of blockade where people go limp and thereby compel the police to have to carry us away. We don't want to call forth hostility in other people. Sometimes people kneel down in the roads to pray. Sometimes we hold up the cross. But when they ask us to stand up, we do so."

I asked Rosemary what she had learned from her years of talking to people whose life's work is linked to weapons. She responded:

"The main thing is not to fear approaching anyone. We need to learn to approach those whom we or others regard as our enemies, whether people in another country or the White House or people anywhere in positions of political or religious leadership—people who have authority and power which could be used for the welfare of the human family. We need to think about the manner in which we approach them. If we can possibly imbibe a little of the spirit of Saint Francis, it will help. He always approached his opponents—even a wolf—in humility but also perfectly confident that he should go. He had a very great simplicity, something that we tend to lack today. We are far too complicated. We need to approach those we are trained to hate or resent or fear, and to do it on a very human level, in a loving way, seeing them, as Francis saw the sultan, as a brother given to him by God. If we can do that, what can we not accomplish?"[66]

What is striking about a person like Rosemary is the modesty and kindness that marks her efforts as a "servant of Christ's peace." She seeks nothing for herself, not even recognition, and is embarrassed on those occasions when she is singled out for attention. She is not undertaking such activities because they are good deeds or a credit to her or to her religious community, but because she has been drawn deeply into God's love and as a consequence sees everyone, even the most difficult or dangerous person, as a child of God, someone beloved of God, someone made in the image of God—even if the likeness is damaged or almost completely hidden.

How desperately we need people like Rosemary, and not only in places where wars are being fought or planned or where weapons are being perfected, but wherever people are targeted, whether in the womb before birth or at any stage along the way. We need servants of peace in our communities, work places, homes, and parishes.

And who is the peacemaker who is needed? It is each of us. The beatitude of peacemaking is part of ordinary Christian life in all its daily-ness.

But serving peace is not easy. Often it is harder to seek dialogue with someone close at hand—a spouse, relative, co-worker, employer, or neighbor—than with a distant enemy seen only on television screens.

In our home, scene of many battles on such monumental issues as television, table manners, dishwashing, length of showers, and cleaning of rooms, it is my wife who deserves a Nobel Prize for peacemaking. She, more than anyone, has helped us talk and listen our way through many squabbles, disagreements, and misunderstandings. Her successes have value not just within our family but dramatically affect what sort of people we are outside the home.

A recent letter from Denise Jillions—office administrator, wife of an Orthodox priest, and mother of three boys—included this observation: "To be a peacemaker, however tiny or great the issue and the stakes—I have in mind one of my sons being willing to let the other pour his orange juice first rather than fight over it—is always heroic, is always reminiscent of the cross and the sacrifice of Christ and his courage to appear weak. He could have called legions of angels to rescue him and fight at the moment, but instead he chose to ask the Father's forgiveness for his enemies. Being a peacemaker is hardly ever popular with people who are sparring to win, it really takes all the 'fun' out of it and can be denigrated as 'wimpy' or foolish. Also, being a peacemaker is different than being an 'appeaser,' not making waves, not standing up for truth. Just as the idea of 'humility' can often be misunderstood as a passive act, so can 'keeping the peace' in a dysfunctional way be confused with being a peacemaker. On the other hand, choosing to deny oneself and avoid a conflict originating in wilfulness and selfishness is also peacemaking or, rather, 'war prevention.' It's a hornet's nest."

Sometimes Christ's peace seems especially absent among his followers. We don't simply disagree with one another on many topics, but we often despise those who hold what we regard as false or heretical views. Disagreement may be necessary—the defense of truth is a virtue—but hatred is a grave sin. Most often it isn't truth we battle for but opinion, vindication of our irritation with someone else, or just the desire to have things our own way. I have seen parishes destroyed over issues that participants five years later were embarrassed to think ever mattered to them, but at the time, there was enough anger to spark a war. That our own parish has held together despite interpersonal friction and a wide range of opinions on potentially divisive issues owes much to quiet efforts made by various individuals, lay and clergy, during periods of tension.

The ear and eye have much to do with peacemaking; the less carefully we listen, the less attentively we see each other, the more likely we are to become embroiled in irresolvable conflict. The phrase *active listening* has taken root in recent years as a way of describing quiet, patient attention to what others say so that the listener can repeat what he or she has heard with such understanding and attention to detail that opponents are certain they have been heard. Such listening can dramatically change the climate and enable real dialogue to happen. Without conscientious listening and attention to the face and other physical attitudes of the other person, dialogue is impossible. What is needed is hospitality of the face and ear.

A still more important dimension of peacemaking is prayer—prayer for enemies, adversaries, opponents, or whomever we fear, find difficult, or wish would vanish from our lives. "The two main activities in peace work are prayer and listening," Rosemary reminds people. "Christ says we must love our enemies and pray for them. The two go together. You will never love anyone you don't pray for. Prayer opens a channel inside us to participate in God's love for the other person."

Far from loving our opponents, as Christ commands us to do, it often happens that we don't even respect them or try to understand them or consider that it may not be they who are wrong. Even if they happen to be dead wrong, there may be ways in which our attitude or response keeps them from changing their mind or way of life.

Our own failure to love is a major part of the problem. As Thomas Merton said in a letter to Dorothy Day:

> Persons are not known by intellect alone, not by principles alone, but only by love. It is when we love the other, the enemy, that we obtain from God the key to an understanding of who he is, and who we are. It is only this realization that can open to us the real nature of our duty, and of right action. To *shut out* the person and to refuse to consider him as a person, as an other self, we resort to the "impersonal law" and to abstract "nature." That is to say, we block off the reality of the other, we cut the intercommunication of our nature and his nature, and we consider only our own nature with its rights, its claims, its demands. And we justify the evil we do to our brother because he is no longer a brother, he is merely an adversary, an accused.
>
> To restore communication, to see our oneness of nature with him, and to respect his personal rights and his integrity, his worthiness of love, we have to see ourselves as similarly accused along with him . . . and needing, with him, the ineffable gift of grace and mercy to be saved. Then, instead of pushing him down, trying to climb out by using his head as a stepping-stone for ourselves, we help ourselves to rise by helping him to rise. For when we extend our hand to the enemy who is sinking in the abyss, God reaches out to both of us, for it is he first of all who extends our hand to the enemy. It is he who "saves himself" in the enemy, who makes use of us to recover the lost groat which is his image in our enemy.[67]

The peacemaker is anyone used by God to help heal damaged relationships. Dorotheos of Gaza, one of the desert saints, used the image of a wheel:

> Suppose we were to take a compass and insert the point and draw the outline of a circle. The center point is the same distance from any point on the circumference. Now concentrate your minds on what is to be said! Let us suppose that this circle is the world and God himself is the center; the straight lines drawn from the circumference to the center are the lives of men. To the degree that the saints enter into the things of the spirit, they desire to come near to God; and in proportion to their progress in the things of the spirit, they do in fact come close to God and to their neighbor. The closer they are to God, the closer they are one another; and the closer they are to one another, the closer they become to God. Now consider in the same context the question of separation; for when they stand away from God and turn to external things, it is clear that the more they recede and become distant from God, the more they become distant from one another. See! This is the very nature of love. The more we are turned away from and do not love God, the greater the distance that separates us from our neighbor. If we were to love God more, we should be closer to God, and through love of him we should be more united in love to our neighbor; and the more we are united to our neighbor the more we are united to God. May God make us worthy to listen to what is fitting for us and do it. For in the measure that we pay fitting attention and take care to carry out what we hear, God will always enlighten us and make us understand his will.[68]

...for they will be called children of God.

Get on board, little children,
There's room for many a more.

—TRADITIONAL BLACK SPIRITUAL

Child of God, therefore children of God, therefore brothers. All
wars are civil wars.

—ERIC GILL

Just as the first part of the beatitude refers to relationships, so does the second. Those who build peace with others are also repairing their relationship with God.

We are so used to praying the Our Father that it doesn't amaze us that we are not only on speaking terms with God but that we speak to God as God's very children. The classical world had a profusion of gods. Mortals could be aware of the deities, imagine their lives, envy their immortality, and try to win the favor of whichever gods might be helpful in times of need. A god might on occasion help or even rescue humankind, as did Prometheus with the gift of fire, yet immortal gods were not seen as humanity's natural allies.

Christ taught that human beings are God's children and that to live in peace with each other as God's children is to live in the kingdom of God.

The foundations for this teaching were familiar to the Jews. The authors of the book of Genesis, with its creation narrative, were less interested in the process of creation than in identifying human beings as uniquely made to live in relationship to God because we are bearers of the divine image. There is noth-

Creation of Adam,
Chartres Cathedral

ing greater. A rabbinic commentary points out that the reason God made only one Adam and one Eve rather than several Adams and several Eves was so that no one could claim to be of a higher descent than anyone else.

"... *for they shall be called children of God.*" The phrase "they shall be called" is a Semitic formula meaning "they shall be recognized as." Those who help establish God's peace—whether preventing war, providing care to those in need, putting two neighbors back on speaking terms, or restoring unity within a family—are recognized as assisting in God's activity in our world. Christ places such people on the highest possible plane, for the peacemaker is doing what God intends. Christ himself is the archetypical peacemaker. As Saint John Chrysostom says in his sermon on the beatitudes: "For this became the work of the Only Begotten: to unite the divided, and to reconcile the alienated."[69]

In Hebrew, a language short on adjectives, a person with a certain temperament might be identified as the "son of" his most notable quality; for example, because of their stormy characters the apostles James and John were called "sons of thunder," and Barnabas was described as a "son of consolation." The translation could also be "children of thunder" or "child of consolation." To say a person is a son or child of God is another way to say he or she is godly.

In the parable of the Prodigal Son, Christ explores the complexity of the relationship between ourselves and God—our human tendency to leave the father's house to live on our own, to waste our inheritance and disfigure our lives until we realize we have forfeited any family claims. He tells a story of rebellion followed by conversion. On the son's side, there is the repentant act of returning; his father—serving as a symbol of God—responds with unreserved mercy, joyfully restoring the prodigal's sonship. The son has recovered, through repentance, qualities he once rejected as childish.

Christ calls on his followers to love their enemies and pray for those who persecute them so that they may be "*children* of your Father who is in heaven, for he makes his sun rise on the evil and on the good and sends rain on the just and the unjust." Just as the weather does not favor the righteous, neither should we love only those who love us, for "even tax collectors do the same" (Mt 5:45-46).

When Christ was asked by his disciples, "Who is the greatest in the kingdom of heaven?" his answer was surely not what they expected. Christ placed a child in the middle of the group and said, "I say to you truly, unless you repent and become like children you will never enter the kingdom of God. Whoever humbles himself like a child is greatest in the kingdom of God, and whoever welcomes one child in my name receives me" (Mt 18:3-5).

The same thread continues in the next chapter of Matthew's gospel with the story of children being brought to Christ so that he "might lay hands on them," that is, give them a blessing. The disciples, in order to spare Christ from what they regarded as a waste of time, tried to stop the parents but were reprimanded by Christ. "Let the children come to me and do not hinder them for the kingdom of heaven belongs to such as these" (Mt 19:13-14). It is for this reason that children are always the first to receive communion in Orthodox parishes.

To live as a child of God is to retain certain aspects of childhood even when your hair has turned grayer than pewter. Nothing is more evident to a child than being in a condition of dependence—autonomy is unthinkable. A child is eager to please its parents and to learn from them. A child is wholehearted in its activities and relationships and pays absolute attention to whatever catches its interest.

Walking in a park near our house recently, I watched a child repeatedly stop to look at flowers in the bushes along the path and each time to show what she saw to her father—luckily he wasn't in a hurry and responded with pleasure. One small, white flower with five petals was enough to stop her in her tracks and fill her with amazement. Thanks to her, for days afterward, walking that path each morning, I took a fresh interest in things I often take for granted.

"The soul of a little child is free from maladies of the mind. He has no memory of wrongs and turns to those who have inflicted them as if nothing had happened," wrote Saint John Chrysostom. "He would rather have his own mother dressed in rags than a queen in all her finery, for a child measures things by love, not by poorness or richness. . . . He looks for no more than is needed. A child who has had enough milk turns away from his mother's breast. He is unmoved by things that upset us, loss of money and so forth; such transitory matters mean nothing to him."[70]

There is a childlike quality in this story of two Desert Fathers who attempted to quarrel:

There were two old men who dwelt together for many years and who never quarreled. Then one said to the other: "Let us quarrel with each other like other men do." "I do not know how quarrels begin," answered his companion. So the other said to him: "Look, I will put a brick down here between us and I will say 'This is mine.' Then you can say 'No it is not, it is mine.' Then we will be able to have a quarrel." So they placed the brick between them and the first one said, "This is mine." His companion replied, "This is not so, for it is mine." To this, the first one said: "If it is so and the brick is yours, then take it and go your way." And so they were not able to have a quarrel.[71]

Blessed are they who are persecuted for the sake of righteousness ... Blessed are you when they insult you and persecute you and utter every kind of evil against you falsely because of me ...

He who does not take up his cross and follow me is not worthy of me.

−JESUS CHRIST (MT 10:38)

What credit is it, if when you do wrong and are beaten for it, you take it patiently? But if when you do right and suffer for it and take it patiently, you have God's approval. For to this you have been called, because Christ also suffered for you, leaving you an example, that you should follow in his steps.

−SAINT PETER (1 PT 2:20-21)

Of course, it would be easier to get to paradise with a full stomach, all snuggled up in a soft feather-bed, but what is required is to carry one's cross along the way, for the kingdom of God is not attained by enduring one or two troubles, but many!

−ELDER ANTHONY OF OPTINA

Having recognized peacemakers as God's children, Christ gives us a double helping of the beatitude of the persecuted. The final beatitude is the longest. It was the Semitic tradition to say anything especially important twice. "Amen, amen, I say to you . . . "

Far from winning applause and peace prizes, those who try to overcome division are often punished, sometimes severely, as many prophets were, as Christ was.

The main symbol of Christianity is not the star of Bethlehem or the empty tomb but the cross. For the ancient Romans it could hardly be imagined that the cross might one day become a religious symbol. The cross in the Roman Empire was what the electric chair, guillotine, and hangman's noose are in our world, except the cross was an especially slow, painful, and humiliating form of capital punishment. The condemned man was stripped of all his clothing. The usual cause of death was not loss of blood but hunger, thirst, exhaustion, and heart failure. Until its abolition by Emperor Constantine in the year 337, crucifixion was used within the Roman Empire to kill slaves, rebels and those condemned for especially abhorrent crimes. The victims were almost always noncitizens of low social rank. In areas like Judea, crucifixion was intended to deter resistance to Roman occupation. After the Roman siege of Jerusalem, many Jews were scourged, tortured, and then crucified opposite the city walls. Josephus says the soldiers "amused themselves by nailing their prisoners in different positions."

Christ repeatedly warned his disciples that he would be killed, a prediction they seemed to ignore. They had witnessed the welcome he received wherever he went and finally his triumphal entry into Jerusalem, with crowds shouting, "Hosanna to the son of David." How could they imagine that only days later he would be dead on the cross and they would be in hiding? Once Jesus was dead and buried, they were not quick to believe the women who were the first witnesses to the resurrection.

What had been a symbol of Caesar's ruthlessness became for Christians the sign of Christ's victory over death. In the Orthodox church it is referred to not just as the cross but "the holy and life-giving cross"–though it didn't look either holy or life-giving at the time of the crucifixion.

After the resurrection the cross was seen in a transfigured light, to the extent that Saint Paul could declare, "Far be it from

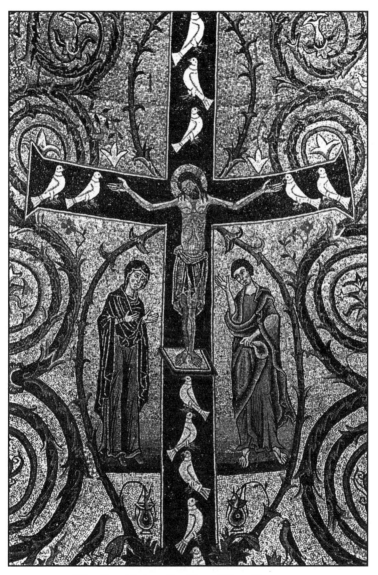

The Crucifixion, Basilica of San Clemente

me to glory except in the cross of our Lord Jesus Christ" (Gal 6:14).

"We must carry Christ's cross as a crown of glory," wrote Saint John Chrysostom, "for it is by it that everything that is achieved among us is gained. . . . Whenever you make the sign of the cross on your body, think of what the cross means and put aside anger and every other passion. Take courage and be free in the soul."[72]

In the same vein Saint John of Damascus wrote:

> Every action . . . and performance of miracles by Christ are most great and divine and marvelous, but the most marvelous of all is his precious cross. For no other thing has subdued death, expiated the sin of the first parent, despoiled Hades, bestowed the resurrection, granted the power to us of disdaining the present and even death itself, prepared the return to our former blessedness, opened the gates of Paradise, given our nature a seat at the right hand of God, and made us the children and heirs of God, save the Cross of our Lord Jesus Christ.[73]

Roman civilization, in general remarkable for its capacity to absorb all sorts of peoples, cultures, and religions, found Christianity indigestible and did its best to destroy its adherents. Those baptized in the first three centuries of the Christian era knew that their conversion would not ease their life in this world. The numerous saints of the early church were all martyrs–from the Greek word *martus*, meaning "witness."

In the early church "martyrdom was the defining characteristic of sainthood," writes Robert Ellsberg.

> Communion with those who had "died in the Lord" was a vivid reality to the early Christians. They liked to gather at the graves of the martyrs to remember their heroic witness and to commemorate the anniversaries of their deaths. . . . The men and women who died in the Roman

arena had offered a total witness to Christ, not only imitating his death on the cross but proclaiming by this sacrifice their faith in the resurrection. Their blood, as Tertullian said, was the seed of the church.[74]

Some martyrs had been exposed as Christians by such actions as refusal to offer incense to Caesar. Others, like Saint George, openly proclaimed their belief in times of persecution; the dragon we see George lancing in the familiar icon represents the beast of fear.

Group identity often centers on a perceived external threat; anyone within the social group who challenges an obligatory enmity will be regarded as a traitor, even if the driving force in his or her life is love of neighbor. I grew up in the United States in a period when "the threat of Communism" affected every social structure. Many people had to sign statements that they were not and never had been Communists—some went to prison for refusing to make such avowals, while thousands lost their jobs and homes because they were regarded as "soft on Communism." Anti-Communism became the country's political bedrock. Toward the end of the Cold War, Georgi Arbatov, an adviser to Soviet leader Mikhail Gorbachev, told a group of American journalists, "We are going to do something terrible to you—we are going to take away your enemy."

Christians were persecuted in the ancient world primarily because they were seen as undermining the social order, despite the fact that in most respects Christians were models of civil obedience and good behavior. Saint Peter called upon followers of Jesus to "be subject for the Lord's sake to every human institution, whether it be to the emperor as supreme, or to the governors as sent by him. . . . Be submissive to your masters with all respect, not only to the kind and gentle but to the overbearing" (1 Pt 2:13-14, 18). Saint Paul wrote along similar lines: "Let every person be subject to the governing authorities. For there is no authority except from God" (Rom 13:1). It must be noted that Paul was himself in prison at the time. He died a martyr's death, beheaded in Rome during the reign of Nero. It was not the view of those who ordered his execution that Paul and his co-religionists were model citizens.

The Christians' great offense was that they held themselves obedient first of all to Christ rather than the emperor. As the martyr Saint Euphemia said: "Both the emperor's commands and those of others in authority must be obeyed if they are not contrary to the God of heaven. If they are, they must not only be disobeyed; they must be resisted." Following torture, Euphemia was killed by a bear in the year 303 during the reign of Diocletian. It was the kind of death endured by thousands of Christians well into the fourth century, though the greatest number of Christian martyrs, mainly Russians, belong to the twentieth century.

People like Saint Euphemia and Saint George were not law breakers in the sense the phrase is usually understood today. Anyone who grew up in the former Soviet Union, however, will understand perfectly well what it is like to live in a society in which not only behavior but beliefs are imposed and in which punishment may be more severe for those whose ideas are unacceptable than for those who steal or commit acts of violence.

Christians resisted the cult of the deified emperor, would not sacrifice to the gods their neighbors venerated, and were notable for their objection to war or bloodshed in any form. In a text written by the pagan scholar Celsus in A.D. 173, Christians were condemned for what today would be called conscientious objection. "If all men were to do as you do," he wrote, "there would be nothing to prevent the Emperor from being left in utter solitude, and with the desertion of his forces, the Empire would fall into the hands of the most lawless barbarians."

It was a reasonable objection, but for the church the example of Christ was paramount. If God wished the Roman Empire to survive, it could better be defended by Christian faithfulness than by disobedience to Christ. The Savior had killed no one, had never blessed any killings, and had said, "Whoever lives by the sword will perish by the sword." Saint Justin the Hieromartyr explains an attitude characteristic of the early church: "We who were filled with war and mutual slaughter and every wickedness have each of us in all the world changed our weapons of war . . . swords into plows and spears into pruning hooks."[75] And elsewhere he writes, "We who formerly murdered one another now not only do not make war upon our enemies but, that we may not lie or deceive our judges, we gladly die confessing Christ."[76]

It is easy to imagine that a community which lived by such values was regarded as a threat by the Roman government. In fact, Christians who live this way today face persecution in many countries. Christianity tends to be tolerated to the extent that it acclimates itself to the society in which it finds itself.

With Emperor Constantine's publication of the Edict of Milan in 313, the first age of martyrdom came to an end. In the decades that followed, what had been the least favored religion quickly became the most favored. Those who had once been threatened with torture and execution were instead threatened with all the material blessings of this world. The emperor's conversion was both a relief and a danger. As Saint Jerome noted, "When the church came to the princes of the world, she grew in power and wealth but diminished in virtue."

It was the age when many Christians, like Jerome and Anthony, fled the cities to live in the desert, thus letting a harsh environment and the demons they met there put them to the test. The Desert Fathers, as they became known, were to provide Christianity with a new wave of saints. Their witness was not facing half-starved wild animals in the arena but struggling to overcome what is beastly in human nature, a kind of combat that in some ways was even harder because the enemy was more intimate. As was often said by Pogo the Possum, a comic-strip character created by Walt Kelly—and one of America's saner voices back in the fifties—"We have met the enemy, and he is us."

In countries where a book like this can be published or sold, there is little danger that the reader will be punished for being a Christian. Does this mean that the eighth beatitude was only for our ancestors or those living in countries where persecution continues?[77]

Perhaps the real question is to what extent we are really living the gospel ourselves. Are we living a timid rather than a meek Christianity? What would happen if we lived our faith with the wholeheartedness and courage that characterized Christians of the first four centuries?

In the Orthodox church, reflection on the beatitudes is often recommended as a way of preparing for confession and communion. Such reflection provides a framework for an examination of conscience about steps not yet taken in our effort to follow Christ:

Do I embrace poverty of spirit—or flee from it at the speed of light?
For whom have I been in mourning?
How meek am I in my response to the gospels?
In what ways am I hungry for righteousness?
How merciful am I regarding those who in some way have done me harm?
How pure is my heart and what keeps it so impure?
In what ways am I trying to purify my heart?
What are the divisions that intersect my life and in what ways am I responding to these divisions as a peacemaker?
What enemies do I love? For which enemies am I praying?
Whose threatened life am I trying to safeguard?
Do I accept persecution as a blessing—or do I avoid anything that might get me into trouble?

If your responses are anything like mine, you haven't just awarded yourself a halo.

What is it that makes us such timid, halfhearted followers of Christ that the last thing we need to worry about is being persecuted on his account?

Part of the answer is that we tend to shape our lives, activities, and vocabularies according to what is more or less "normal" where we happen to live. Social creatures that we are, we unconsciously adjust our practice of Christianity to fit within the limits imposed by the society we live in, with further adjustments geared to our social and working lives. I am made aware of the tension of being a Christian in a secular society through the embarrassment I have to overcome every time I start to read the Bible or a clearly religious book in a public place.

I first became conscious of how readily we conform our responses to others around us when I became part of the Saint Joseph's House of Hospitality in New York City. Among our weekly activities was handing out a mimeographed leaflet critical of preparations for nuclear war. Three or four of us would stand for an hour at midday on corners in midtown Manhattan near an office responsible for "civil defense," the organizing center for all that New Yorkers were obliged to do in preparing for a nuclear attack. Once a year a civil defense drill was imposed on the city; stopping every car and bus and requiring everyone to take shelter in basements and subway stations. The world's busiest city briefly became a ghost town.

Handing out our leaflets, we were like children exclaiming that the emperor was naked. You won't survive nuclear war by taking shelter in the subways, our text pointed out; but if you do, you will find yourself in a world resembling hell.

What an education it was watching people on a busy city street. New York's traffic-light system being what it was, people came down Lexington Avenue in waves. I learned that the response of the first person in each group—invariably a man in a hurry—usually determined the response of everyone who happened to be following him. Not a word was said, not a look was exchanged—the process was automatic and unconscious. If I could get the man in front to take our flyer, at least some of those behind him were likely to follow his example. If he refused, the chances were that no one would accept the piece of paper I was offering.

I began to notice the same phenomenon in other settings and finally to discover it in myself. Making conscious use of this principle is called leadership.

In many ways we human beings swim in schools no less than fish do. It is for this reason that perfectly ordinary and decent people living in Germany in the thirties and early forties found themselves cheering Hitler, obediently playing their part in invasions of neighboring countries, killing people they had no personal grudge against, and assisting the Holocaust. Among Christians in Germany and Austria there was relatively little resistance to Nazism, though it was a period not without saints who risked and often obtained a martyr's death.

I recall an experience related to me by Hildegard Goss-Mayr, a courageous Christian whose peace work has saved thousands of lives and inspired many to struggle against injustice using nonviolent methods. She told me about the one occasion in her life when she saw Adolf Hitler. It was 1938 in Vienna. Though only twelve years old, thanks to her parents she had a clear idea of who Hitler was and what the Nazis stood for. Her father was head of the International Fellowship of Reconciliation, a post Hildegard would occupy later in life.

> All the students of the city were brought out to one of the main roads to welcome him and I was one of those in that big crowd. And there I was, on my own. Then the convoy of cars appeared and there was Hitler standing in one of them. Everyone around me was lifting their hands and shouting, *"Heil Hitler! Heil Hitler!"* It was the first time that I felt that there really is a strength of evil, something that is stronger than any individual being. I experienced the fascination that came from Hitler, that manipulation of masses of people. Evil can have a tremendous attraction. I knew I was not allowed to lift my hand or to join in the shouting. I thought, "Even if they kill me, I am not going to lift up my hand."
>
> It was extremely hard. It was a personal decision at that moment to stand against it. It was an important moment of struggle within myself, a struggle with violence, and a struggle with justice and truth and love. It was a

struggle that, in a way, wounded me. Not only that day but in the years that followed, this struggle continued with great intensity. When I was seventeen, I felt that I could not go on living if men behaved so terribly toward each other. It touched even my willingness to live. It marked my soul. From seventeen until I was nineteen, I really had to struggle, to make a choice to go on living, to find the will to live. But then I could build on the little seed that my father had planted, his belief in the power of love, that God has given us the vision of the unity of life. But throughout my life I have been very sensitive to the force of evil and have had to struggle with despair.[78]

Hildegard's story reveals another aspect of what makes so many of us carefully avoid the beatitude of persecution: *fear.*

In his essay "The Root of War Is Fear," Thomas Merton noted that it is not so much the fear people have of each other "as the fear they have of everything. It is not merely that they do not trust one another; they do not even trust themselves. . . . Only love—which means humility—can exorcise the fear that is at the root of war."[79]

I mailed Merton's essay to my father, who soon after responded with appreciation but said he could not agree. "The root of war," he said, "is bad economics." Years passed without either of us mentioning Merton's essay. I only discovered he had continued thinking about it when I received a letter in which he told me, "I have come to realize that the root of bad economics is fear."

Not only war and social injustice but any failure in moral life, private or collective, has something to do with fear. On the one hand, there is fear of social rejection, with all its potentially dire consequences. On the other hand, there is also fear of God. Truly, it is a fearful thing to fall into the hands of the living God. Probably every reader of this book believes in God, at least as a principle of creation. It is unlikely that any of us holds creation responsible for creating itself. We have at least an intellectual sense of God's existence, even if we see God as a force as impersonal as gravity. One can believe in gravity without feeling the slightest obligation to love gravity or to respond to gravity with prayer. Intellectual belief is one thing, devotion is another. Love is an attitude at the core of being. To love and not be willing to sacrifice for those one loves is a contradiction in terms. Love is always a willing surrender of autonomy. As Christ observed: "Greater love has no one than this, than he lay down his life for his friends" (Jn 15:13).

It need not be actual death that love requires, but love is always a dying to self—even such small dyings to self as Denise Jillions describes at the family breakfast table—one son allowing the other the first glass of orange juice. What often keeps us from making even such modest gestures is fear of being thought weak.

Each of the beatitudes has to do with dying to self.

Poverty of spirit, the foundation of the beatitudes, is the ongoing process of dying to self, not out of self-hatred or a collapse of self-esteem, but because there is no other way to love God and neighbor.

It is a subject Father Thomas Hopko, Orthodox theologian and dean of Saint Vladimir's Theological Seminary, often speaks about:

> The obsession with relationship—the individual in search of relationships—in the modern world shows that there is an ontological crack in our being. There is no such thing as an individual—he was created, probably, in a Western European university. We don't recognize our essential communion. I don't look at you and say, "You are my life." . . . The only way we can find ourselves is to deny ourselves. That's Christ's teaching. If you try to cling to yourself, you will lose yourself. And of course, the unwillingness to forgive is the ultimate act of not wanting to let yourself go. You want to defend yourself, assert yourself, protect yourself, and so on. There is a consistent line

through the gospel—if you want to be the first you must will to be the last. . . .

There is no self there to be defended except the one that comes into existence by the act of love and self-emptying. It's only by loving the other that myself actually emerges. And forgiveness is at the heart of that. . . . I have no self in myself except the one that is fulfilled by loving the other. The Trinitarian character of God is a metaphysical absolute here. God's own self is another—his Son, to use Christian evangelical terms. The same thing happens on the human level; so the minute I don't feel deeply that my real self is the other, then I'll have no reason to forgive anyone.

But if that is my reality, and my only real self is the other, and my own identity and fulfillment emerges only in the act of loving the other, that gives substance to the idea that we are potentially God-like beings. Now, if you add to this that we are all to some degree faulty, weak, and so on, that act of love will always be an act of forgiveness. That's how I find and fulfill myself as a human being made in God's image. Otherwise, I cannot. So the act of forgiveness is the very act by which our humanity is constituted. Deny that, and we kill ourselves. It's a metaphysical suicide.[80]

Many of the traditions of spiritual life that have developed within Christianity are intended to help that dying to self that Christ describes as poverty of spirit. Fasting is one of these traditions—a small dying to certain foods and drinks. The chief value of fasting is not dietary but is linked to intensified battle against the tyranny of one's never satisfied appetites and desires. Fasting is always linked with increased prayer and almsgiving: the deepening of communion with God and with neighbors in need.

A mother of three recently told me how she looks forward to the four long fasts that are part of the church calendar (the fast of Saints Peter and Paul at the beginning of summer, the Dormition fast at the end, the nativity fast in the weeks leading up to Christmas, and the great fast before celebrating Christ's resurrection). "During these times," she says, "life at home is always more peaceful. Probably it's partly just chemical—the children get less sugar—but it's also a change in everyone's attitude."

Mourning is also a surrender of self. In the grief of never again seeing in this world someone who has died, there is a deep realization of the infinite value of other lives and the certain knowledge that I am nothing if not in communion with others.

Meekness is dying to self—a surrender to God and a surrender to the needs of those whom God has given us to love and serve.

Hungering and thirsting for righteousness requires dying to self in the daily struggle to overcome in oneself and in society all those things that keep us apart from God and from each other, everything that destroys communion and community.

Being merciful is a surrender to God, another dying to self. It is not my own personal mercy I have to offer, only God's mercy passing through my life—if only I will get out of the way.

A pure heart is unobtainable except through death to self. The only thing that makes a heart pure is God's presence in the heart.

Peacemaking is also a death to self. There is no peace without risk to the self in trying to safeguard the legitimate needs of others, whether friends or enemies. Consider Saint Francis, first facing a wolf and then seeing to it that the wolf was cared for.

Accepting persecution as a blessing is the final act of death to self—a poverty of spirit that allows us to cope with condemnation and rejection without bitterness and hatred.

It is all these surrenderings of self to God, most often in very tiny actions invisible to others, that make up the ladder of the beatitudes.

... for theirs is the kingdom of heaven. ... Rejoice and be glad, for your reward will be great in heaven, for so men persecuted the prophets who were before you.

Was there ever a prophet whom your fathers did not persecute?
–SAINT STEPHEN, THE FIRST CHRISTIAN MARTYR (ACTS 7:52)

We claim that we desire the kingdom of God, and yet we neglect those things that ensure we could gain entry there. And although we make no efforts to fulfill the Lord's commands, we still imagine in our foolishness that we will receive the same honors as those who have fought against sin right up to their death.
–SAINT BASIL THE GREAT, *THE LONGER RULES*

In the final beatitude, Christ singles out the prophets as models.

Prophets are probably not the kind of people you would want to invite to a birthday party or whom any parish I know of would wish to have preaching every Sunday. They have never been well-behaved people who carefully follow the social guidelines laid down by Emily Post and Amy Vanderbilt and their predecessors. In their urgent efforts to pry open closed eyes and ears in order to inspire repentance and conversion, they have shouted, ranted, and sometimes behaved in bizarre ways. As Rabbi Abraham Heschel wrote: "To us a single act of injustice—cheating in business, exploitation of the poor—is slight; to the prophets, a disaster. To us injustice is injurious to the welfare of the people, to the prophets it is a deathblow to existence; to us, an episode; to them, a catastrophe, a threat to the world. . . . They speak and act as if the sky were about to collapse because Israel has become unfaithful to God."[81]

A prophet is a person speaking and acting on God's behalf; the Greek word is *prophetes,* "someone who speaks before others"; the Hebrew word, *nahi,* means "person called by God." In various biblical texts the prophet is described as a watchman, a servant, and a messenger of God. "His true greatness," Rabbi Heschel remarked, "is his ability to hold God and man in a single thought."[82]

Prophets would not do well in any line of work that required them to say, "It's not your fault. You don't have to call it a sin—just a mistake. God could expect no more of you." The prophets never substitute evasive words for direct words. They have no interest in excuses. They warn their listeners that God scorns our religious activities unless they are supported by a just life:

> I hate, I despise your feasts,
>> and I take no delight in your solemn assem-
>>> blies.
> Even though you offer me your burnt offerings of
>> your fatted beasts,
>> I will not accept them. . . .
> Take away from me the noise of your songs. . . .
> But let justice roll down like waters,
>> and righteousness like an everflowing stream.
>>> (Am 5:21-24)

This is not to say that the biblical prophets were unbearable people who have been honored after burial but were never listened to. They made a life-changing impact on many people, high and low, who saw them face to face. Their way of speaking made them hard to ignore. In the prophetic books in the Bible we notice that their language was not only passionate but

poetic, and that their desperation—Jonah being the one exception—is linked with love, not misanthropy. If the mouth of the
prophet is "a sharp sword," as Isaiah says, it is the surgeon's
scalpel meant to save life, not the razor of a Jack the Ripper.

Among the primary themes of the prophets is indifference to
the suffering of the poor and becoming wealthy at their expense:

> [The rich] drink bowls of wine
>> and anoint themselves with the finest oils,
>> but they are not grieved for the affliction of
>>> Joseph. (Am 6:6).

> "Woe to him who heaps up what is not his own!
>> . . .
> You have brought shame to your house
>> by cutting off many people
>> and have sinned against your soul.
> For the stone cries out from the wall
>> and the beam from the woodwork replies.
> Woe to him who builds a town with blood
>> and founds a city on iniquity!" (Hb 2:6, 10-12)

> They [will survive all trials] who walk righteously
>> and speak uprightly,
>> who despise the gain of oppression,
> who wave away a bribe instead of accepting it,
>> who stop their ear from hearing of bloodshed,
>> and shut their eyes from looking on evil.
>>> (Is 33:15)

> They have cast lots for my people and have sold a boy for
> prostitution and a girl for wine, that they might drink.
>> (Jl 3:3)

> Hear this, you who trample upon the needy
>> and bring ruin to the poor of the land,

saying, "When will the new moon be over
    that we may sell grain
and the Sabbath
    that we may offer wheat for sale,
making the ephah small and the shekel great
    and falsifying scales by deceit,
that we may buy the poor for silver,
    and the needy for a pair of sandals,
and sell the refuse of the wheat?" (Am 8:4-6)

The prophets classify sins against the poor as acts of disobedience to God, who does indeed regard us as responsible for each other. After Cain killed Abel, he said to God, "Am I my brother's keeper?" The implications of the story go beyond one person striking a deadly blow. Because I am my brother's keeper, whatever I do or fail to do that contributes to the death of another makes me an accomplice in murder. As Isaiah warned:

How is the faithful city become a whore!
    She was full of justice.
Righteousness lodged in her,
    but now murderers. (Is 1:21)

Not only those who personally commit acts of evil are implicated in the sins of society. Jeremiah says that even the prophet denouncing sin shares in the guilt:

Run up and down the streets of Jerusalem.
    Look and take note!
Search the squares to see
    if you can find a man
who does justice
    and seeks truth. . . .
Everyone is greedy for unjust gain,
    from the prophet to the priest. (Jer 5:1, 8:10)

Again and again rulers were among those called to account by the prophets. During the reign of King Ahab, Elijah opposed Queen Jezebel's promotion of the cult of Baal, an offense that put his life in danger. It was while he was in hiding that Elijah heard God's whisper. Later, having accused Ahab of complicity in the murder of a neighbor whose vineyard he wished to possess, Elijah said Ahab's descendants would be destroyed and that Jezebel would be devoured by dogs, a prophecy that stirred Ahab—but sadly not Jezebel—to repentance. Jezebel did not die a happy death.

Because the prophets were often bearers of news that no one wished to hear, they often became targets. Jeremiah predicted the Babylonian defeat of Israel and the leveling of Jerusalem. His dire warning provoked deadly hostility. After prophesying the destruction of the Temple, he was tried for blasphemy. On another occasion, at the king's orders, he was flogged and put in the stocks. Jeremiah saw Israel's downfall not in geopolitical terms but as God's punishment for the disobedience of God's covenanted people.

There was nothing politic about the way Jeremiah addressed King Johoiakim. He told him that no one would mourn his death: "With the burial of an ass he shall be buried, dragged and cast out beyond the gates of Jerusalem" (Jer 22:19). Jeremiah avoided arrest and possible execution by going into hiding. Later he was imprisoned in a cistern, where it was intended he would starve to death, though at last the king ordered his release. Following the fall of Jerusalem, Jeremiah went into exile in Egypt where, according to legend, he was stoned to death after protesting idol worship by other Jewish refugees.

The prophets anticipated the coming of the messiah. Isaiah declared that a daughter of the House of David "would conceive and bear a son and will call him Emmanuel [God with us]" (Is 7:14). Isaiah is responsible for these consoling words:

> The people who walked in darkness
> have seen a great light . . .

The rod of the oppressor
   will be broken . . .
Every garment rolled in blood
   will be burned as fuel for the fire.
For to us a child is born,
   to us a son is given,
and the government will be upon his shoulder,
   and his name will be called
Wonderful Counselor, Mighty God,
   Everlasting Father, Prince of Peace.
Of the increase of his government and of peace,
   there will be no end. (Is 9:2, 4, 5-7; see also 11:1-9)

The last of the prophets, John the Baptist, was a "voice crying in the wilderness" calling his fellow Jews to a baptism of repentance and promising that "all flesh shall see the salvation of God" (Lk 3:4, 6). He was so obedient to God's will and so quick to respond that in icons he is often shown with angel wings (the Greek word *angelos,* means "messenger"). John urged tax collectors, notorious for their greed, to take no more than was appointed and told soldiers not to rob or make false accusations and to be content with their pay. It was John who saw a dove descend on Jesus at his baptism and heard a voice from heaven say, "This is my beloved Son." Like the prophets before him, John did not hesitate to accuse rulers. Having chastised Herod "for all the evil he had done," John was imprisoned and finally beheaded.

There was little joy and much suffering in the prophets' lives, yet the ladder of the beatitudes ends with Christ's summons to rejoice because, along with the prophets, "your reward will be great in heaven."

In a culture notorious for its impatience, in which delaying gratification is not what we are best at, the idea of rejoicing now for what will happen later is not easily adopted.

On the other hand, *not* to live by the beatitudes makes me think of a *New Yorker* cartoon of a young couple being shown a house that is nothing more than a castoff army tank. "It's a little small inside," the real estate agent admits, "but you can't beat it for security."

Following Christ is not the choice to make for anyone whose goal in life is security. You had better buy the tank. The windows are tiny and there is no guest room, but it will probably keep out thieves. You will have the well-guarded if lonely feeling of being in a safety deposit box inside a bank vault.

When I think about films that have mattered in my life, "Last Holiday" is on the short list—an ironic British comedy written by J. B. Priestly and released in 1950. Alec Guinness plays George Bird, a salesman as cautious as a civil servant, who has never married because what women see in his face is dread of life, not an attractive quality. A persistent headache has made him consult a doctor. After medical tests, Bird has been told to come back the next day for the diagnosis, but by the time he returns the files have been mixed up. The doctor has someone else's results in Bird's folder and so informs him that he has an untreatable illness and will be dead in six weeks. In fact, all Bird needs is an aspirin or perhaps a pint of beer.

The doctor's error transforms Bird's life. He quits his job that very day, empties his bank account (there is no longer any point in saving up for old age), and books a room in a luxury hotel, a coastal resort for the affluent. He had never imagined setting foot in such a place until he spotted the graveyard racing toward him. A day later he begins his last holiday. No longer needing to play it safe, Bird can say and do things he previously would never have dared—there is nothing left to fear. For the first time in his life women find him attractive. Bankers, corporate executives, and government ministers are soon lining up for his advice, offering partnerships and vice-presidencies. Everyone senses in him a mysterious quality, a detachment and freedom that make him a figure to be reckoned with. The viewer alone knows just what that mysterious quality is: Bird's death sentence has been his liberation. He is no longer a prisoner of the terrifying future.

The people in the hotel are far from a happy group. In many ways their holiday hotel is a well-appointed purgatory. Bird becomes something of a Saint Francis in his efforts to help his fellow guests become less selfish people, though it takes only his being late to a meal in his honor to sour their affection for him. What they don't know is that the guest of honor has just been killed in an auto accident while off on a mission of mercy. The doctor with the wrong file was right after all, not in his diagnosis but in the basic fact that George Bird—not to mention every one of us—is going to die and there's nothing we can do about it. The physician's only error was that it took less than six weeks to happen.

If it were in my power, I'd include a video of "The Last Holiday" with every copy of this book. It's a film about poverty of spirit: stepping into a life in which I am no longer in charge, in which I own nothing, in which, like George Bird, I am freed by news of my own death. Free as a bird.

It is also a film about overcoming fear. What keeps us from the beatitudes is fear—fear of others, fear of the contempt of our peers, fear of being a social castaway, fear of poverty, and ultimately, fear of death.

Another way of expressing the same thing is to say that we are people of little faith. "If you had faith even the size of a mustard seed," Jesus tells us, "you could move mountains" (Mt 17:20). Christ wasn't referring to Mount Sinai or Mount Tabor but to more intimate obstacles: our mountains of caution and disbelief, our mountains of fear.

The main word in the beatitudes is *blessed.* Truly they are blessed who are poor in spirit, who mourn, who hunger for righteousness, who are merciful, who are pure of heart, who make peace, who are as willing as the prophets to risk punishment for the sake of God's kingdom.

But there is another word in the beatitudes that lights up the text: *rejoice.*

If there is no God, or if God has no interest in the activities of creatures that happen to exist on particular planets, it hardly

matters who we are, what we do, or what we believe. We are on our way to the dust bin where the dust of Stalin is indistinguishable from the dust of John the Baptist.

But if the gospel is true, if the truest thing we can say is that God is love, if following Christ is the sanest and wisest thing we can do in our lives because each step forward brings us closer to the kingdom of God, then we have much to rejoice in. We hear that rejoicing in a canticle-like vision of Bridget of Kildaire, one of the great saints and mystics of Ireland:

> I should like a great lake of beer for the King of
>   Kings.
> I should like the angels of Heaven to be drinking it
>   through time eternal.
> I should like excellent meats of belief and pure
>   piety.
> I should like flails of penance at my house.
> I should like the men of heaven at my house;
> I should like barrels of peace at their disposal;
> I should like vessels of charity for distribution;
> I should like for them cellars of mercy.
> I should like cheerfulness to be in their drinking.
> I should like Jesus to be there among them.
> I should like the three Marys of illustrious renown
>   to be with us.
> I should like the people of heaven, the poor, to be
>   gathered around us from all parts.

Those who climb the ladder of the beatitudes are in the best of company: the prophets, the martyrs, and the saints–the great cloud of witnesses.

Notes

1. Later Iona was home to a Benedictine abbey. While there has been no monastic foundation on the island since the Reformation, the abbey ruins have been rebuilt by the Iona Community and now serve as a conference and retreat center.

2. John Climacus, *The Ladder of Divine Ascent*, trans. Colm Luibheid and Norman Russell (New York: Paulist Press, 1982), 30th step, 5.

3. Oliver W. Sacks, "The Lost Mariner," *The Man Who Mistook His Wife for a Hat* (New York: Simon & Schuster, 1987), 23-42.

4. *Butler's Lives of the Saints*, ed. Herbert Thurston, S.J., and Donald Attwater (New York: Kenedy & Sons, 1963), 3:609.

5. Harold Isbell, personal communication. He noted the word's adaptation by America's "beat generation" of the fifties: "Allen Ginsberg and Jack Kerouac saw 'beat' as a shortening of 'beatific.'"

6. Benedicta Ward, trans., *The Wisdom of the Desert, Apophthemegmata Patrum*, rev. ed., intro. Anthony Bloom (London: Mowbray, 1984), xiv.

7. See the chapter on holy fools in Jim Forest, *Praying with Icons* (Maryknoll, N.Y.: Orbis Books, 1997).

8. Thomas Merton, *The Wisdom of the Desert* (New York: New Directions, 1961), 41-42.

9. *Francis and Clare: The Complete Works*, trans. and intro. Regis J. Armstrong, O.F.M.Cap., and Ignatius C. Brady, O.F.M. (Ramsey, N.J.: Paulist Press, 1982), 152.

10. Leo the Great, Homily XCV, "On the Beatitudes."

11. John Chrysostom, "On 1 Corinthians," XXI, 4.

12. Yevgeny Yevtushenko, *A Precocious Autobiography* (New York: Dutton, 1963).

13. Climacus, *The Ladder of Divine Ascent*, 7th step, 145.

14. Glinda Johnson-Medland, "Grieving under the Protecting Veil," *In Communion*, journal of the Orthodox Peace Fellowship, issue 4, March 1996.

15. Fyodor Dostoevsky, *Crime and Punishment*, trans. Richard Pevear and Larissa Volokhonsky (New York: Knopf, 1992), 460.

Notes

16. Fyodor Dostoevsky, *The Brothers Karamazov*, trans. Richard Pevear and Larissa Volokhonsky (New York: Knopf, 1990), 289.

17. John Chrysostom, *Sermons on Matthew*, IV.

18. *The Sayings of the Desert Fathers: The Alphabetical Collection*, trans. Benedicta Ward, rev. ed. (London: Mowbray, 1984), 138-39.

19. Helen Waddell, *The Desert Fathers* (Ann Arbor: University of Michigan Press, 1966), 121-22.

20. Ward, *The Sayings of the Desert Fathers*, 129-30.

21. *Martin Luther King: A Documentary*, ed. Flip Schulke (New York: Norton & Co., 1976), 25.

22. Augustine, "On Our Lord's Sermon on the Mount," sermon 3.

23. John Chrysostom, *Sermons on Matthew*, XV.

24. Ward, *The Sayings of the Desert Fathers*, xxi.

25. John Chrysostom, *Sermons on Matthew*, XV.

26. Leo the Great, Homily XCV.

27. William Blake, "Auguries of Innocence."

28. Father Serge Hackel has written an excellent biography of Mother Maria. See *Pearl of Great Price* (Crestwood, N.Y.: Saint Vladimir's Seminary Press, 1981).

29. Thomas Merton, *The Sign of Jonas* (New York: Harcourt, Brace & Co., 1953), 362.

30. Flannery O'Connor, "A Memoir of Mary Ann," pages 830-31 in *Collected Works* (New York: The Library of America, 1988).

31. Alexander Solzhenitsyn, *The Gulag Archipelago* (New York: Harper & Row, 1974), vol. 2, part 4, "The Ascent."

32. Archimandrite Sophrony, *The Monk of Mount Athos: Staretz Silouan 1866-1938*, rev. ed. (Crestwood, N.Y.: St. Vladimir's Seminary, 1973); Archimandrite Sophrony Sakharov's writings on the life of Saint Silouan, as well as the texts Staretz Silouan wrote himself, are available in a single volume, *Saint Silouan the Athonite*, published by the Monastery of Saint John the Baptist (Tolleshunt Knights by Maldon, Essex CM9 8EZ, England).

33. John Chrysostom, *Sermons on Matthew*, XV.

34. Dostoevsky, *The Brothers Karamazov*, 352.

35. Isaac of Syria, *Directions on Spiritual Training*, Test 85.B, no. 8.

36. Oscar Wilde, *The Ballad of Reading Gaol* [1898], pt. V, Saint 14.

37. Antoine de Saint-Exupery, *The Little Prince* (New York: Harcourt Brace Jovanovich, 1971), chap. 21.

38. Homer, *The Iliad*, trans. Richmond Lattimore (Chicago: University of Chicago Press, 1951), bk. IX, 1.312-13.

39. William Shakespeare, *King Henry the Sixth*, Part II, Act III, Scene ii, line 232.

40. John Donne, *Holy Sonnets*, no. 14, 1.1.

41. William Blake, "The Divine Image," st. 3, in *Songs of Innocence*.

42. *The American Heritage Dictionary*, 3d ed. (Boston: Houghton Mifflin Company, 1992).

43. Boris Vysheslavtsev, cited in J. B. Dunlop, *Staretz Amvrosy* (Belmont, Mass.: BVA Books, 1972), 22.

44. Seraphim of Sarov, "Spiritual Instructions for Laymen and Monks," first paragraph. The principal writings of Saint Seraphim, including the "Spiritual Instructions," are available in *The Little Russian Philokalia*, vol. 1: St. Seraphim, 3d ed. (Platina, Calif.: St. Herman Press, 1991).

45. I am aware of two biographies of Seraphim of Sarov in English: Valentine Zander, *Saint Seraphim of Sarov* (Crestwood, N.Y.: Saint Vladimir's Seminary Press, 1975); and Iulia de Beausobre, *Flame in the Snow* (London: Constable, 1945; since reissued by various publishers).

46. For further reading, see A Monk of the Eastern Church [the pseudonym of Father Lev Gillet], *The Jesus Prayer* (Crestwood, N.Y.: Saint Vladimir's Seminary Press, 1987); and Bishop Kallistos of Diokleia, *The Power of the Name* (Fairacres, Oxford: Convent of the Incarnation, 1986).

47. Isaac of Syria, *Ascetic Treatises*, 85.

48. The complete text of this story is included in Waddell, *The Desert Fathers*, 75-76.

49. Isaac of Syria, *Ascetic Treatises*, 81.

50. Solomon Volkov, ed., *Testimony: The Memoirs of Shostakovich* (London: Faber & Faber, 1981), 38.

51. Ibid., 40.

52. Ibid.

53. Ibid.

54. Ibid., 41.

55. Ibid., 148-49.

56. Ward, *The Sayings of the Desert Fathers*, 160.

57. The full text of Motovilov's conversation with Saint Seraphim, found and published only after Saint Seraphim's canonization in 1903, is included in *A Treasury of Russian Spirituality*, comp. and ed. Father George Fedotov (New York: Sheed & Ward, 1948; reissued Belmont, Mass.: Nordland Publishing, 1975; originally published Gloucester, Mass: Peter Smith, 1969).

58. C. S. Lewis, *The Great Divorce* (London: The Centenary Press, 1945), 63.

59. Ward, *The Sayings of the Desert Fathers,* 3.

60. *Spiritualité Orientale* (Bellefontaine Abbey, France); in English, *The Roots of Christian Mysticism,* trans. Olivier Clément (London: New City, 1993), 273.

61. Lev Gillet, *Serve the Lord with Gladness* (Crestwood, N.Y.: Saint Vladimir's Seminary Press, 1990), 15.

62. Luke's version of the text–12:51–uses "division" rather than "sword."

63. Arnaldo Fortini, *Francis of Assisi* (New York: Crossroad, 1981), 216.

64. For a detailed account of Francis's trip to Egypt, see Fortini, *Francis of Assisi,* 395-439.

65. *Fioretti,* XXI; a detailed treatment is in Fortini, *Francis of Assisi,* 535-39.

66. The interview with Sr. Rosemary Lynch was published as "A Franciscan in the Nuclear Age" in *Reconciliation International,* the journal of the International Fellowship of Reconciliation (November 1987), 8-11.

67. Thomas Merton, *The Hidden Ground of Love: Letters of Thomas Merton* (New York: Farrar Straus & Giroux, 1985), 140-43. Extracts from letters Merton wrote on peacemaking are included in Jim Forest, *Living with Wisdom* (Maryknoll, N.Y.: Orbis Books, 1991), 149-55.

68. Dorotheos of Gaza, "On Refusal to Judge Our Neighbor," *Discourses and Sayings* (Kalamazoo, Mich.: Cistercian Publications, 1977), 131-39.

69. John Chrysostom, *Sermons on Matthew,* XV.

70. Ibid., LXII.

71. Ward, *The Sayings of the Desert Fathers,* 299.

72. John Chrysostom, *Sermons on Matthew,* LIV, 7.

73. John of Damascus, "Concerning Faith and Baptism," *An Exact Exposition of the Orthodox Faith,* bk. 4, chap. 9.

74. Robert Ellsberg, *All Saints* (New York: Crossroad, 1997), 1.

75. Justin, *Trypho,* CX.

76. Justin, *I Apol.,* XXXIX.

77. Countries in which it remains dangerous to be a Christian include Sudan, Saudi Arabia, Egypt, Iran, China, North Korea, and Laos. Among groups trying to respond to the danger is Christian Solidarity International, whose work includes ransoming enslaved Christians in Sudan.

78. The interview was published in *Reconciliation International,* the journal of the International Fellowship of Reconciliation (November 1988). For detailed presentation of Hildegard Goss-Mayr's life and thought, and that of her husband, Jean, see Gérard Houver, *A Nonviolent Lifestyle: Conversations with Jean and Hildegard Goss-Mayr* (London: Lamp Press, 1989).

79. Thomas Merton, *New Seeds of Contemplation* (New York: New Directions, 1961), 112, 119.

80. Thomas Hopko, *In Communion,* the journal of the Orthodox Peace Fellowship, issue 1 (Spring 1995), 1-5; also posted on the Orthodox Peace Fellowship web site:

http://ourworld.compuserve.com/homepages/jim_forest/hopko.htm

81. Abraham Heschel, *The Prophets* (New York: Harper & Row, 1962), 21.

82. Ibid., 5.